There Aren't Any Kitchens in Heaven

By

Claudia M. Jones, Ph.D.

© 2002 by Claudia M. Jones, Ph.D. All rights reserved.

No part of this book may be reproduced, stored in a retrieval system, or transmitted by any means, electronic, mechanical, photocopying, recording, or otherwise, without written permission from the author.

ISBN: 1-4033-8407-X (e-book)
ISBN: 1-4033-8408-8 (Paperback)

Library of Congress Control Number: 2002095130

This book is printed on acid free paper.

Printed in the United States of America
Bloomington, IN

1stBooks - rev. 03/25/03

Acknowledgments

I would like to thank my loyal friends—and loyal you are—who have known me through the years and never questioned me...only listened and cared. You are true friends and I appreciate all you've done for me.

Special thanks to my niece Jennifer, Lisa Wells, and Dan Geoghegan, who read my work and provided invaluable input for my mind, heart, and writing.

Thank you, Lisa Veilleux, for editing my work with such care. Your sensitivity and understanding allowed the process to be painless.

My thanks, also, to all those who taught me to tack. Your encouragement enabled me to sail into the wind, and taught me that a zigzag course is sometimes better than a straight line. You helped keep the music of the wind in my sails.

Dedication

To my mother, who is the most influential and powerful individual in my life, I thank you for all the wealth you gave me that could never be found in material possessions but rather within the heart and soul of your very being. Your love allowed me to reach for the stars, while your encouragement and unselfish nature, which taught me more than any text book could offer, enabled me to catch them. You will never know the difference you've made in all the lives you've touched, and so on behalf of all of us, I thank you. You are truly an amazing woman!

To my five children whose mere existence makes my life complete, I thank you for being the joys that fill each and every moment with an unexpected surprise. You captured the child in Paul and somehow managed to enable him to forget the larger scope of life and focus on enjoying the moment. You seized his kinder side and unconditionally loved him, always. For that, I am eternally grateful.

To my husband, I thank you for believing in me through it all. Your acceptance of Paul and genuine concern for him amazes me. You managed to alleviate much of his stress through your humor, patience, and love.

To my brother Paul... I'm so very sorry you suffered and missed so many of the simple pleasures of life. I certainly wish I could have done more and I wish it could have been different for you. Though you suffered tremendously, you never complained even once, and for that you have my total admiration. Maybe one day it will all make sense. I certainly hope so. May God bless you, today, tomorrow, and always. I do love you.

"For of all sad words of tongue or pen,
The saddest are these: 'It might have been!'"
—John Greenleaf Whittier

TABLE OF CONTENTS

Acknowledgments	iii
Preface	xi
Introduction	xiii

Part One: Paul's Story

Chapter 1. Nature and Nurture	3
Chapter 2. Signs and Portents	13
Chapter 3. Sound and Fury	25
Chapter 4. Faith and Hope	49

Part Two: A Mother's Story

Sofia Maurer's Journal	55

Part Three: The Doctors' Story

Psychological Evaluations	97
Epilogue: By Sofia Maurer	121

Preface

While teaching a graduate course at a university in Florida, I assigned outside readings to fulfill a course assignment. Specifically, students were to read biographies, autobiographies, or memoirs of individuals who fit into various "exceptional" categories. Upon reading the students' book reviews, I realized I had a contribution to make. I am the sister of a man diagnosed with paranoid schizophrenia. This is his—our—story. The names of my family, our friends, some hospitals, and all doctors, attorneys, and judges have been changed.

I write this book to give an insider's view of life with a mentally ill family member—to provide a firsthand account of its devastating effects, both on the afflicted individual and on the family who loves him.

Introduction

He was discontented and restless for days, spending both his working and sleeping hours locked in his room. The days melted into weeks and his connection with reality grew ever more tenuous. He had separated himself from the world, from life. The door was kept shut, whether to lock us out or to lock his highly pressurized feelings in, we didn't know. Lying on his unmade bed, he listened to pounding, angry music on the radio beside his dresser and smoked pack after pack of cigarettes.

As the smoke wrapped him in a veil of gray, swirling around and over his head, his thoughts were dark and terrifying. A lifetime of oppressed feelings had grown to terrifying proportions. In his mind, his mother hated him, wished to rid herself of him, would send him away—maybe forever. In his mind, he saw himself an outcast, being dragged, kicking and screaming with tears streaming down his face, to the ambulance.

He imagined that his mother stood there, hands on hips, smiling as she made the final arrangements with the hospital personnel. His mother's hollow eyes looked at him as she made hollow promises: You'll feel better.

You'll get well.

PART ONE
PAUL'S STORY

"I do not understand what I do.
For what I want to do I do not do, but what I hate I do."
       — Romans 7:15

CHAPTER 1
NATURE AND NURTURE

My Ukrainian mother and Irish-German father did not have an ideal marriage. My dedicated mother ran a perfect household, seemingly without effort, but labored through her marriage, hoping against all odds that the dysfunctional union would flourish. It did not. My mother is an extremely generous woman, who gave until there was nothing left to give in her efforts to change a failing marriage.

It wasn't an easy task to live with a man who thought—who honestly believed—he was never wrong. My father enjoyed martinis and beer nightly, and took money out of my mother's weekly allowance if she failed to mail a birthday card to one of his family members, if dinner was late, or if the food was not cooked to his favor. My mother's lot was not a happy one, but not once did her family hear of her unhappiness, even though we felt it.

I was the youngest child of four and the only girl, which had numerous advantages and disadvantages. Owing to my father's mercurial nature, I was never "Daddy's little girl" but, rather, Phillip, Dan, and Paul's little sister. I don't recall much of my earlier years, but, as family lore has it, having a girl after three boys was pure icing on the cake for my parents, which may be why I was never addressed or spoken to in a belittling manner by my father, as my brothers regularly were.

Claudia M. Jones, Ph.D.

When I was born, Paul, until then the baby, had an extremely challenging time adjusting. I am certain that, with any effort, my father could have made the transition easier for the five-year-old, but no such effort was made. As my father proudly showcased his daughter, Paul clung to his trousers for any display of affection, but all silent pleas for recognition went unnoticed. Who knew then that Paul's silent, unanswered cries would eventually explode into a nightmare for one and all?

Paul's insatiable desire and need to be heard only increased with time. He was always the rambunctious child, the one who was the most curious, and definitely the one who, as a young child, required the majority of my mother's time. My mother tells the story of how she had to feed Paul in his highchair since he couldn't sit still. He would try to climb out of the highchair, so my mother would brace him with her forearm and shovel food in with her other, spoon-equipped hand. This feeding ritual was repeatedly practiced and must have been quite exhausting for my mother.

Since my two older brothers, Phillip and Dan, were already in school, my mother was able to attend to Paul and his numerous needs. He was quite creative and enjoyed playing "Pomato Boy" with my mother for hours. He would put tomatoes in a basket, knock at the door, and to my mother's inquiry of "Who is it?" would reply, proudly and matter-of-factly, "It's your Pomato Boy!"

When I was less than a year old, our family life was disrupted when my father announced that we would have to move to Mexico for a year so that he could earn his doctorate. My mother packed us all up and off we drove to Guadalajara, Mexico. We spoke no Spanish and knew absolutely no one. My brothers left their schools and my mother left her family and friends, all to appease her husband's need to succeed.

I have no memories of Mexico due to my age at the time; I celebrated my first birthday there and we returned to the States shortly thereafter. I do know that the conditions under which we lived were totally unlike those we were accustomed to in the United States. Although we all gave up something, my mother sacrificed everything. But the tiny woman accepted the challenge and acted in good faith.

She made certain our lives were filled with all the essentials necessary and all the luxuries possible. Although money was tight, the six of us had an overall successful year as we tried to conform to an unfamiliar culture and, simultaneously, hold on to our roots. My brothers harbor the images of our life in Mexico; to this day, my brother Dan recalls having his favorite jacket stolen there. He was heartbroken, as was my mother, but both accepted that they would never see the treasured jacket again... until the day of a traditional parade, in which Dan spotted a fellow classmate marching proudly, wearing the jacket he took from his *gringo* peer. Displaying the resolve which was one of the traits of his German heritage, Dan marched right alongside the Mexican and removed the jacket from his body in full view of the spectators.

Paul's memories of Mexico seem to be particularly painful, and most involve my father. One Sunday morning, prior to Mass, my father disciplined Paul so severely that when the family attended church, the natives inquired as to what happened to Paul's eye. I imagine seeing a six-year-old with a shiner seemed unusual to them. My mother replied honestly, "His father hit him." One can only imagine what people thought of us. Needless to say, we were glad when my father finished his studies and we could leave Mexico.

The return home symbolized, I am certain, hope of a new beginning for both Dr. Phillip J. Maurer and his wife, Sofia. But symbolism varies from individual to individual, and such subjectivity can be met with strong opposition. And, from my recollection, it was indeed so.

When we returned to the United States, Paul attended parochial school along with his two older brothers. It was a tremendously difficult adjustment for both mother and son due to the incredible bond they shared. It was an arduous task for my mother to pull Paul off of her daily when it was time for school. She had attempted to serve as a sanctuary, both physically and emotionally, for the son she sensed was different. Paul often clung to his mother with a tremendous amount of fear and uncertainty, but especially love. Our mother was Paul's mainstay, always. He adored her, worshiped her, and clung to her, pleading to return home to play Pomato Boy—a game which would no longer be played, except in their minds and hearts.

A reverent altar boy with a crew cut and adorable Dopey ears, Paul could charm his way into anyone's heart... anyone's, that is, except his father's. Paul's second grade teacher, Mrs. Murphy, thought he was an amazing student, especially when he sang "If I Could Talk to the Animals" from Dr. Dolittle. Mrs. Murphy recognized Paul's need for attention and willingly obliged, moving his desk right next to hers. There was, without question, an extremely sensitive side to Paul. But just as strong was the side which was a confused little boy with confused little thoughts and ideas, waiting to be exposed.

If I could have bottled and sold the energy in Paul, I would be wealthy. More often than not, he was the troublemaker on the school bus or the practical joker who was out to get a laugh, even at the expense of an innocent bystander. He picked on kids and provoked numerous fights for no apparent reason except the one in his mind, which was his driving force. Although as his younger sister I would have been an easy target, surprisingly Paul never vented his hurt, anger, or frustration on me. He did, however, channel his energies to others.

He was active within our neighborhood, playing sports, riding his bike, and fishing at the lake at the end of our block. But he also found tremendous satisfaction in throwing rocks at the conductor of the train that passed by daily in the afternoon. This angered the conductor greatly—so much, in fact, that one day he stopped the train and chased Paul and another neighborhood boy for blocks. Eventually, the boys were caught and, as a punishment, the neighbor's father beat his son daily with a belt when the train whistle blew. It was during the winter months when there was no need for air conditioning, so the windows were wide open. The boy's bloodcurdling screams seemed to travel and visit all the surrounding houses. My mother never disclosed Paul's actions to my father, likely from fear of his retribution.

We ate dinner together as a family every evening. My mother cooked the most delicious dinners, but the company was never good when my father joined us. He would raise his voice constantly at my brothers. I can still close my eyes and hear my father's sharp tongue and sarcastic wit badgering his sons during our family dinners. I hated it, yet never expressed disapproval to my father.

In addition to being a wonderful cook, my mother has a soprano voice that mere words cannot describe. It was always a treat when she sang us to sleep each night. She instilled in us her love of music by involving us in Ukrainian folk dancing, which celebrated her Ukrainian heritage, and by making sure that we all had piano lessons. My father—who had never taken a piano lesson in his life, but nonetheless knew it all—felt compelled to supervise my brothers' practice. He would stand over the boys, ruler in hand, and would hit their knuckles if they were not turned properly. The tears streamed down, and the practice went on, and on, and on.

My brothers would sometimes attempt to stand up to our father, to no avail. I once witnessed my father throw my brother Phillip, then fifteen years old, down the full length of the corridor of our 5,000 square foot house, out the garage door, and up against the side of the car. When my father then balled up his fist, I gasped. He turned around and, meeting the look of disbelief on my face, walked back into the house, sparing Phillip temporarily.

One year Paul planned a surprise birthday party for my mother. As hard as he tried, nothing seemed to go as poor Paul planned, and his first attempt at the party failed when my maternal grandmother blew the whistle. His disappointment devastated him. Even though I was quite young at the time, I will never forget the image of my brother sprawled across two kitchen chairs face down, sobbing as though a death had taken place. His lanky body shook for hours as the tears slid down the chair and hit the floor. But, luckily or unluckily for Paul, his second attempt at a surprise party was successful—due in part to his not inviting our maternal grandmother, or any other family members outside our own household, for fear that someone would betray his secret.

The family was gathered in the family room, watching television, when the first knock sounded. Paul grinned. A dear friend of my mother's was the first to arrive, present in hand. Everyone was speechless, and I can still feel the heat of alarm that traveled through my body as I realized what was happening. If only the five-year age difference between Paul and me hadn't seemed so vast at the time, perhaps he would have confided in me, and I could have helped him plan the party. There was nothing to serve the guests—no special food or drinks, or other supplies necessary for entertaining. The only ingredients we had for a party were many guests, presents, and my irate father with his terrible temper. I can so vividly recall him scrunching up Paul's shirt in his left hand, balling up his right hand into a fist in Paul's face, and whispering, "If you ever pull something like this again I'm gonna kill you." And, to prove his credentials, he released Paul with a shove that toppled the birdcage. I wonder what the guests thought? My beautiful mother thanked Paul a million times, but I don't think it compensated for the threat imposed by my father.

There is a part of me that truly believes Paul was glad to have pleased my mother. But an even bigger part of me believes that Paul was glad to have annoyed and aggravated my father, who spoke to no one for days following that episode.

The rate of unfortunate incidents escalated as time passed.

I remember one evening Paul, who was sick, walked across the kitchen floor with a thermometer in his mouth. He fainted in midstep, but my father did no more than glance over to where Paul lay, then returned to reading the paper and sipping his spirits.

Sometimes, after dinner, the neighborhood kids would gather in the street to play. On one of these evenings, my father was napping—whether due to a hard day at work or the alcohol he'd consumed, I'll never know. Unfortunately, our playing woke him and, before I knew it, my mother was giving me a bath and sending me to bed for the night at seven o'clock. Even at my young age, I understood enough to ask why she had ever married him. She paused, then answered, "I don't know."

Although they hardly spoke, decisions were made that affected us all. I was evicted from my bedroom so my father could occupy it, while I slept with my mother. He remained in my room, and I in his with my mother, for two years. During this time, he didn't speak one word to my mother. When communication could not be avoided, he wrote notes to her. My mother was solely responsible for all of our care; my father effectively abdicated all parental responsibility. My mother did everything for us, including driving us all to school—three different schools, at one point—while my father forbade any of us to ride in his car or boat.

My mother is a devout Catholic; her faith has been the foundation of her strength in managing the difficulties of her life, as well as a source of comfort and hope when all seemed hopeless. Her dedication to her Catholic faith also made her determined to uphold the holy vows of matrimony in a marriage which would have tested the devotion of any saint. But ultimately, she did ask my father to leave. His *written* response to her request said that he would.

The final family dinner—The Last Supper—took place when I was seven years old; Paul was twelve, Dan was fourteen, and Phillip was sixteen. My mother served her usual, carefully prepared five-course meal. My father cut into a baked potato and said, "This is hard." This proclamation was made with incredible intensity and, therefore, warranted strong and immediate action. He threw down his utensils in utter disgust and stormed out the front door, my mother following with me in tow.

"Don't leave like this," she called. "Don't just walk out. Let's talk about this."

His final word to her, which I will forever recall, was *"Bitch!"*

He sat in his convertible Spitfire and sped away, never looking back. I know; I stood in the driveway and watched.

* * * * *

Not long after that terrible night, I came home from a neighbor's house to find my father loading up the family station wagon. Not understanding the true nature of my parents' problems, I assumed we were going camping. I bypassed my father and met my mother in the utility closet as she handed my brother Phillip some necessities my father might need. She had a sad, yet determined, look on her face. I was told to go outside and play. It was clear we were definitely *not* going camping.

Then I saw Paul. He had a fit, yelling at me in the middle of the street, "Why did you tell the neighbors that Mom and Dad are getting a divorce?" I had no idea what the word even meant, but I knew it had to be important because Paul was holding a wet face cloth and patting his face, which was as white as the marshmallows we'd toasted around family campfires in better times. His marble-blue eyes were lost and he sobbed uncontrollably. Unsure of what to do, I stood in the driveway and watched as my father loaded his television, clothes, and other belongings into the station wagon with the greatest of care. Too bad he couldn't handle his family with such care.

But my mother possessed a tremendous reserve of strength, which was never more evident than in a crisis like this one. I know the tears she cried when my father left were for us. How in

God's name was she going to keep the house and raise four children ages sixteen, fourteen, twelve, and seven?

She took a job immediately, because we certainly weren't going to survive on my father's child support. He refused to pay any support for Phillip and Dan because they worked part-time for a construction company and he felt they would do fine. Paul and I received money contingent upon our weekly visits to his house. Neither Paul nor I wanted to visit, but we really had no choice—if we didn't, my mother didn't receive her check. What else could we do?

My father possessed idiosyncrasies that were difficult to comprehend, let alone accept. For example, on our birthdays my mother would want to bring us to relatives' homes for parties, while my father thought we should, instead, go fishing with him. When offered the choice of presents or fishing, we naturally chose the party. This infuriated my father to the point that he alienated us during all holidays; we were forbidden to call him on any holiday until we reached eighteen years of age. My two older brothers didn't care, and I was too young to understand how deranged his actions were, but Paul was very affected yet again. He needed my father, but that need was never met.

Amazingly enough, given my mother's financial situation, the four of us remained in parochial school. Paul played the trumpet in the school band; the two of us were in a Christmas concert together one year. Along with three others, I was to open the show with a Christmas Eve tableau. The nuns told us all to wear pajamas in order to add reality to the scene. Little did the nuns know that my mother had bought me the brightest dress in town—pink with silver glitter all over, and I do mean *all* over. It even came with a matching purse. She was quite excited, and I had no intention of revealing the truth to the nuns about my planned attire. In fact, I managed to run late for the show so I wouldn't be sent home to change. I arrived fashionably late in my glittery pink dress, matching purse, frilly socks, and patent leather shoes, and will forever remember the looks on the nuns' faces and their dour inquiry: "Miss Maurer, are these pajamas?" It was much too late to do anything except remove my shoes and sparkle away! Seeing the glow of pride on my mother's face (or maybe it was merely the reflection of the glitter from my dress) was well worth disappointing the nuns.

There Aren't Any Kitchens in Heaven

My father never attended any of our events, but it really didn't matter because my mother compensated in every way. I never missed my father, but Paul felt his absence keenly. My mother once received a phone call from Paul's English teacher, who was concerned about something Paul had written as an assignment. The work was entitled "Someone I Admire," and although most of the boys described their fathers, Paul described our neighbor, Jim Kiick, who played football for the Miami Dolphins. In great detail, Paul described how Jim Kiick devoted time to his son, was a wonderful father, and how Paul wished he, too, could have some type of relationship like the one he saw in the Kiick house. It was beyond touching. Paul so badly wanted a relationship with a father who made no attempt whatsoever to be one, and Paul bore the scars of that disappointment for the rest of his life.

In his desire to be part of a "complete" family, Paul formed a close friendship with a family in our neighborhood, a young married couple with two small boys, when he was around twelve years old. But he was disappointed yet again when the family moved to South Carolina; he missed them terribly.

He continued his involvement in neighborhood activities, with music, and as the very best Ukrainian folk dancer in his age group. He was proud of his ability to thrill an audience with his steps. On weekends Paul would often stay at the home of a fellow folk dancer who was his best friend. He also loved to polka, and at the dances, known as *zabavas*, all the girls his age would compete to dance with him, he was that good.

But despite his accomplishments, the eighth grade was difficult for Paul, and it was apparent to all, especially to my mother, that Paul was in dire need of medication to control his behavior. One psychiatrist prescribed Ritalin, which made my mother happy—she knew Paul was suffering, as was she. But when my mother disclosed this remedy to the nuns, they strongly dissuaded her from using drugs as an intervention, encouraging her, instead, to rely on faith that God would change Paul's behavior. But, much to our dismay, He didn't. And so the suffering continued.

In the years since, my mother has been left wondering what might have become of her darling Pomato Boy had she listened to the psychiatrist instead of the nuns. No one will ever know the answer, and the question continues to plague her.

CHAPTER 2
SIGNS AND PORTENTS

As Paul entered high school, older brothers Phillip and Dan were both doing extremely well in school, and I was in the fifth grade. Perhaps the parochial, all-boys high school that my mother had planned for Paul to attend would have been better for him, but it was not to be. While boarding the school bus, Paul exchanged words with the principal and "accidentally" pushed him, causing the principal to trip on a rock and fall backwards. The principal had a close relationship with our family, and the matter probably could have been resolved privately had not the entire school bus of students witnessed the incident. In accordance with school policy, Paul was expelled and off to the local public high school he went.

My mother was not sure what to do about Paul and his "incidents." At the time they occurred, the inconsistencies of his behavior compared to that of others were probably largely dismissed with the old adage "Boys will be boys." My other brothers were busy with college and work, so their perception of the situation was limited. I was far too involved with cheerleading and my friends to take note. My mother diligently attempted to hold it all together, but often, Paul was on his own. And on his own was usually not a good place for Paul to be.

There were other times, though, when Paul would show himself to be mature and responsible beyond his years. When he was fourteen, a visit was arranged to the neighborhood family he'd befriended a few years earlier, who were now living in South Carolina. He arrived to find that the young couple, whom he'd imagined having the perfect marriage that had eluded his own parents, had just separated. In an attempt at reconciliation, the wife went to meet with her absent husband, leaving the two young children with Paul, who she hurriedly instructed to take the boys up the hill to their grandmother's house. Paul did as he was told, but was surprised and unsure of what to do when the grandmother—who had apparently not been consulted about the plan to care for her grandchildren for an undetermined length of time—did not welcome either Paul or her grandsons into her home. So Paul took the boys back to their house, climbed through an open window, and cared for the children himself for a week until their mother returned. She was shocked to learn what had transpired while she was gone, and was extremely grateful for what Paul had done. But Paul had learned from my mother's example that whatever the circumstances, caring for and about people comes first.

When he returned to school that fall, both Paul and my mother found high school devastating for him, both academically and emotionally. Paul was working part-time in construction, but the unstructured public school environment provided him the freedom to follow a pathway of bad experiences. If he wasn't suspended he was often skipping school, at home watching detective stories.

Even Paul's well-intentioned undertakings earned him only trouble, such as the time he decided to have a plant sale. The night before the big event, Paul was out in front of our house, smoking a cigarette, when a police car drove past. Paul claimed that he couldn't sleep and that there was nothing wrong with smoking a cigarette at three o'clock in the morning in front of his own house. But the two officers in the car were suspicious nonetheless and, Paul claimed, played with his mind. He would later recount the bizarre event in the following journal entry.

After watching rock concert I was to excited to sleep because of my plant sale so I went outside to finish painting a plant sale sign and other stuff.

There Aren't Any Kitchens in Heaven

When I was done I went out in the street, right outside our house, to smoke a cigerete. I just lite a cigerete when a car came rolling around the corner at high speed. I thought it was just a roddy kid. But just then he slammed on his brakes. A policeman jumped out. He pused me against the car and started to search me. While he was I said 'What did I do wrong?' He said 'Don't give me that shit. I saw you running from the school' and I said 'What school? Hey man I don't know what your talking about.' He checked my cigerette box for pot and took off my hat to check it. He said 'Get in the car' and I said 'But I did not do anything. I live right here,' and he said 'Sure.' So I got in the car. While we were driving to the school I said 'But I did not do anything' and he said 'Shut up.'

Well we got to the school. As soon as we got there they had one kid. I went up to him and said 'Hey man do you know me?' and he said no but they did not believe it. So I got in the car with the other kid. The police that picked me up said 'I got him over by 14th Street.' They were talking about what to do when they got off of work. One said 'The gaters haven't been fed for along time.' So they got me out of the car. Well they ask me if I have ever been arrested and I said no and they said 'Don't give me that bullshit.'

One police told me to drop my jacket and hat so I did. Another police said 'Your mom has to wash your clothes. Pick them up,' so I did. The first police came up to me and said 'Drop them,' but I said no. 'I said drop it' the first police said, but I said 'The other officer told me to pick it up.' He said 'Drop it' in an angry voice but I said no. So he grabed my left hand and bent it up my back and choked me and at the same time throuh me on top of the car and I said 'OK man OK.' But then he through me on the ground and rammed his knee in my back and graped my left hand and put the cuff so tight that the next day there were marks all over my rists.

Claudia M. Jones, Ph.D.

> *I was on my stomach and he said 'Get up' and he would not help me. They gave me my rights. Then they put me in to the car. They were talking and I heard him say 'That juvenille deligent, that wise ass.' They were nicer to the kid they caught then me. Then they got me out of the car and I said 'Hey man can I say something,' and he said 'Don't call me man.' And I said 'I swear I had nothing to do with this.' One of them said 'We are going to give a little slack this time if you promise not to do it any more.'*
>
> *Well I wasn't going to argue with them so I said OK. So they took my cuffs off and took my name, address, telaphone, and my mother's name. They shinned the light on my hands and there was black paint on my hands from the plant signs. And the cop who throw me on the ground looked at his shirt and said 'You better not have gotten any on me.' I said one thing, 'I did not even come close to this school' and one cop said 'Shut up or I'm going to hit you on the hand with this flashlight,' swinging it in my face.*
>
> *They said that I owed an apology to the police that threw me on the ground so I said 'I'm sorry.' They said 'Get going,' and I ran all the way home.*

One day around this time, I heard a knock on the door and, much to my surprise, saw a few policemen waiting outside. I was certain they weren't there to play Pomato Boy! Paul had been spotted, on various days and by various neighbors, breaking into homes. My mother was aware of this, because she was the one who placed the call to the police. She planned to confront Paul, with the police there to back her up, and approach the neighbors with an offer of restitution. But her plan failed as the police handcuffed Paul and put him in the back of a police car. I screamed for them to release him, but my pleas did not move the officers.

I turned to my mother and followed her to her bedroom, where she focused on a tiny, empty jewelry box. Her one reminder of her ex-husband and of a once-special dream had been stolen. Her wedding ring, a beautiful solitaire, had been pawned. As she tried to suppress her emotions, I thought how tiny and empty she appeared at that moment.

My mother dropped the charges against Paul and he was released, but over time, she noticed that other valuables were taken. Little did we know at that time that this behavior was an early manifestation of Paul's mental illness, and merely the beginning of all that we would eventually endure.

* * * * *

When a Ukrainian folk dancer turns sixteen he is sent to camp in Kerhonkson, New York, to attend Ukrainian cultural courses for two weeks. As he was constantly in trouble by age sixteen, this trip was a much-anticipated break for both Paul and my mother. At the camp, Paul would be in a stimulating cultural environment with teens of Ukrainian heritage from all over the United States and Canada. We all were excited for him and prayed that he would fit in and make friends. But any aspirations we had for Paul in this regard faded when my mother received the inevitable phone call. Due to Paul's misbehavior, failure to adhere to rules, and abuse of alcohol, he was being flown home only days after arriving. My mother hung up the phone, sighed, and walked away. Life goes on, and so it did.

While at camp, Paul did meet a girl from Texas. A few weeks later he asked her if he could come to visit. His reputation had evidently not preceded him there, as the family consented. My mother, ever the optimist, was waiting for something to work out in Paul's life. Perhaps a girl, and a Ukrainian one at that, would be the answer. Off he went. As the days of his visit went by, Paul seemed to be productive and under control. The girl's father was able to find him a job in a factory. Paul was thrilled. But his good fortune was short-lived; as he was working, the tip of the middle finger on his right hand was severed. He returned home.

Paul's education meant nothing to him, so he dropped out of high school and decided to join the Marines. No doubt part of his reason for choosing that particular branch of service was to impress his father, an ex-Marine himself. First, however, it was imperative that Paul obtain a high school diploma. The Marines assured him it wouldn't pose a problem. They provided Paul with a GED test book, which, when completed successfully, would earn him a high school diploma. While Paul sat at our dining room table one evening, completing the assignment, he stumbled upon something truly amazing: The answers to all the problems were located in the back of the book! After emitting an exclamation of joy, Paul leaped up and phoned his recruiter with his discovery. Yes, that was fine, the recruiter assured him, not to worry, just take the GED test as he was doing. Paul obliged and, thanks to Uncle Sam, possessed a high school diploma within weeks. *The few, the proud, the Marines*, indeed.

We were all quite hopeful that Paul would do well in the military. He craved a challenge, was somewhat aware that he lacked discipline, and was certainly in dire need of a change. But when the Marines arrived unannounced at four o'clock in the morning, he turned to my mother and sighed, "Mom, I'm not so sure I want to do this." The poor woman! Poor Pomato Boy!

But Paul followed through with his commitment to the Marines and actually flourished in boot camp. My mother would have given anything to see him graduate, but was unable to afford the trip to Paris Island, South Carolina, to witness the event first-hand. However, she and I did meet Paul at the airport with great excitement and anticipation upon his return. My mother was positively glowing with pride and carried a huge bag of confetti with which to celebrate Paul's achievement. But when Paul walked off the plane he seemed tense—there was no smile, no joy, and when my mom threw confetti on him he snapped at her to stop. Paul was struggling to make the transition from boyhood to adulthood, and having his mother throw confetti on him in public was not part of the plan. He was so angry his face was red, and I could feel my heart beating right out of my chest as an unwelcome thought materialized: Like father, like son. I was afraid and most uneasy as the three of us drove home in complete silence.

My father was so proud of Paul that he took him, together with Dan and me, out to eat in an elegant restaurant. He did not extend the invitation to my brother Phillip, who had long since ceased to have anything to do with his father. My father ordered Paul a beer, but the waitress asked to see Paul's identification. My father, belligerent with happy hour spirits, raised his voice and made a scene. How was it that his son the Marine, all decked out in dress uniform, could be old enough to defend our country but not old enough to drink a beer? What kind of country did we live in? Dan attempted to calm the situation by ordering a beer and winking toward Paul and my father, but not much more was said at our "celebratory" dinner, except that my father would take Paul to the Playboy Club for a more fitting celebration before he left town. Paul was elated.

Paul wore his dress uniform the night my father picked him up to be wined and dined at the Playboy Club. It is impossible to express how much this gesture of my father's pride in him meant to Paul. He returned home with a picture of himself, in full dress uniform, between two beautiful bunnies. The picture captured what was to be Paul's first, and last, proud smile for a very, very long time.

Paul's leave was up and he returned to Uncle Sam a real Marine—with a Marine's salary. Paul was generous with his bounty, sending money to my mother, or to me in a card, instructing me to use it to "help Mom around the house." It reminded me of the days when, as kids, Paul and I went to the weekly kiddie show movies. We had just enough money to get in, but nothing for goodies. But Paul would fix that by opening the exit door from inside so I could sneak in, and we'd share popcorn with my money. There definitely existed a tender side of Paul, even if it wasn't exposed often.

But in spite of what he shared with us, the money Paul now earned was, for him, like the key to a Pandora's box of illicit pleasures. Alcohol, drugs, and gambling all became obsessions. Paul recognized that he was having trouble and turned to his trusted confidante—my mother. I remember he began calling home at some very irregular hours. I would walk into the kitchen and hear my mother speaking softly, her face showing great concern. Usually within hours after these calls, my mother was speaking to our great-uncle, a priest in Canada.

In addition to his new compulsions, the rigid structure of the military and the discipline imposed by overbearing superiors were unbearably frustrating to Paul. The pressure became too great one day when, as a training exercise, Paul and his fellow Marines' barracks and lockers were torn apart and they were given a limited time to put everything back together again. Paul simply left. He took a friend and headed for Canada, where he knew he'd find sanctuary at the home of our great-uncle the priest. He stayed there, frightened, for as long as he could.

Claudia M. Jones, Ph.D.

With the combined efforts of my mother and my great-uncle, Paul was able to work out a deal with the Marines—if Paul and his buddy returned, they would receive a "general under honorable" discharge, and no punishment of making little rocks out of bigger rocks would be imposed. Paul was a Marine from April 1976 to July 1977, but returned home with nothing to show for the experience but some new compulsions and a bitter attitude, which he later expressed in the following journal entry.

> *Before I went to my recruiter, I was an informant or C.I. for vice or vind. So I thought I would go see my recruiter, I would be a demalision expert for the Marine Corps. When I got out I would go to work for D.E.A., or the F.B.I., where my uncle, William Maurer, is the head of, in a city in Pennsylvannia, till he got transferred recently.*
>
> *So I went to my recruiter, and he garenteed me that I would be a demalision expert. He said that it came under 'Zullue Tour.'*
>
> *I was in boot camp on free time, and I headed straight for maratorious P.F.C., I was high shooter at the rifle range the first day. I told a friend what I was going to be, M.O.S., and he asked me how old I was. I said 17 and he said you had to be 21 years old. So I asked my drill instructor if that was true and he said yes it was. I was so pissed off that the next day I blow up at my drill instructor when they were playing fuck-fuck as they called it. So they threw me out of the platoon and transferred me to another platoon in the same series. I even came in first place in the first three mile run.*
>
> *Every time the drill instructor, in the other platoon, had a talk with us, whenever he would say something they didn't understand, he would point at me and say 'Maurer understands, don't you?' and I say, 'Yes.' When we were on mess-duty, a bunch of us got caught smoking cigaretts with some Marines that were stationed there. Well we got caught and when our senior drill instructor asked who was*

smoking, I was the only one to admit it. I told him the truth and at the end he loved me for it.

Once out of boot camp I got in all kinds of trouble. Off hours, I seemed like evry week. My C.O. asked me if I wanted to see a syciatrist but I said no. I even tried to kill myself with drugs once cause I hated the service so bad for what they did to me.

Then I decided I could make my glands in my neck swell up, like I had mumps. So I use to use that whenever things got too rough, which is crazy enough. Then they finally decided it was that I was ellurgic to something. When I use to be in isolation for suposofully having the mumps I use to try to break my knee cap with a piece of wood cause I had enough of the service by now. And again I thought I could get a medical discharge for a busted knee cap which I never could do, but still have trouble with now.

I've tried to get into two drug programs now and both won't take me cause they say I use drugs for madisanal purposes. Headace's from the service.

Then I went out one night and tore up the base with my car, and ended up on 'C' row. I was in jail less than a week and they pulled me out and said that if I plead guilty about the 7 or 8 charges they would give me a good discharge. Write about now I needed a lot of scycological help. I saw my chaplan and told him I couldn't take it any more but he said too bad.

So I plead guilty and got discharged in four days. I got out of the service and was so happy to get out I was able to keep things together for about a year. Then I started taken drugs and was so unhappy because of what my recruiter did to me. I started hearing voices and they said they were C.I.T, which is like the C.I.A. or F.B.I. in savilian world. I haven't worked now in over three years and am in bad shape. I still hear voices and they tell me I'm a spy, and stuff like the bar *Rizzo's* I go to is under federal jurisdiction, which it is cause I've asked one

> *of the owener's. I cann't stand life and feel the service owe's me retroactive pay from when I aplied three years ago. I'm still an informant for D.E.A. and try my best, but I just can't work.*

* * * * *

Paul had worked part time as a carpenter in high school, and now resumed that work in his area of specialization—he was a wonderful stonemason. Somehow he was able to recruit workers and, together with his motley crew, made a name for himself. Given his growing drug use, how fitting was the name he chose for his new enterprise: Stoney's Masonry. Paul and his crew built fireplaces and brick walls, laying bricks as fast as they could. Word of mouth spread fast, and they built a superior clientele.

But the success of Stoney's Masonry overwhelmed Paul. Most of the money he made was spent on alcohol and drugs, including PCP or "angel dust"—known to induce a psychosis similar to acute schizophrenia. As a result, he began to miss work and shun his responsibilities. After a meteoric rise, Paul's success was rapidly dissipating. His crew was frustrated with his new attitude and left, one by one, as they found employment elsewhere. Paul was left with no workers, no jobs, nothing but the urge to get wasted at every opportunity.

He tried to get money any way he could, to satisfy his addictions. Paul owned a beautiful blue truck but, wanting to receive insurance money, painted it and set it ablaze in our front yard. Luckily, the house was spared because all the fire trucks arrived in time to suppress the blaze. Dan noticed that the vandalized paint found on the truck matched a can of paint from our garage. Unfortunately, the discovery was made in front of the police, and Paul was a suspect. No insurance money, no truck, and no explanation as to what was happening to Paul.

He himself often seemed as perplexed by his inexplicable actions as we were. From what we could see outwardly, it simply appeared that Paul was a very troubled—and troublesome— young man. What we couldn't see was that inwardly he was fighting a daily and escalating battle against an invisible enemy. Perhaps in response to his experimentation with the powerful hallucinogenic PCP, or perhaps just because it was time, the illness that had lain dormant within Paul all his life had risen up and had begun to wage its relentless, covert war for the control of his mind.

CHAPTER 3
SOUND AND FURY

I awoke from a fitful, worried sleep to the insistent barking of the neighborhood dogs. I drew the curtains, looked outside, and saw Paul. I smiled as our German Shepherd, Bacchus, loped happily near his limp hand. Nothing was amiss, yet something seemed wrong. I put aside my uneasiness and started my morning shower.

I was interrupted a few minutes later by a knock at the front door, where our neighbor stood stolidly, looking grim. I glanced next door to his house and saw patrol cars and police. The neighbor's van tilted lopsidedly in his driveway, three of its four tires flat—slashed, he informed me, by Paul. Paul, wild-eyed and gesticulating violently, screamed to the police, "I didn't do it! Their cousin wants me to narc on my friends! He wants me to work with him and now he's out to get me!" Paul repeatedly denied the charges, but his wild behavior was carefully noted by the police. A yellow Camaro pulled up to the scene: my father and his new wife. He and my mother conferred with the police, and it was decided that Paul would be taken to the veterans hospital for observation.

At the hospital, Paul broke away from the admissions office and ran down the antiseptic halls, muttering that they were all out to get him. My father, who'd managed to distance himself from any involvement in Paul's problems since the day he'd walked out, now looked distraught. I felt like we were in a scene from *One Flew Over the Cuckoo's Nest*. My mother followed Paul's fleeing figure until he reached the street. He stopped suddenly and followed my mother placidly inside, blaming his father for all the inconsistencies and disappointments of his life. For the past several years, Paul had moved further and further beyond our comprehension, but at that moment I understood him completely, and my heart went out to the repentant "child" embraced tightly in my mother's arms.

Later, my mother and I went next door to apologize to the neighbors. With our emotions still running high from the day's tribulations, it was hard to face their callous attitude—all they cared about was the money we owed them. They'd already contacted a tire company to arrange for the specific replacements they wanted, and demanded their money *now*. As worried as we were about what was happening with Paul, it was difficult to accept that they were much more concerned about their tires than they were about my brother.

We returned home silently. That night as I lay in bed, my stomach turned as I mulled over the events of the past few days. I thought of Paul, of my father, of my mother. I thought of the neighbors. It all seemed to me like a play, tangible and real before my eyes, but not reality. There were good characters pitted against bad characters, with Paul in the middle—a victim of circumstance mired hopelessly in his own disintegrating world. As I lay in my comfortable bed at home, I imagined him that night, his transparent blue eyes flickering beneath their delicate lids as he slept among the truly insane. For the first time I wondered: Was he one of them?

* * * * *

My mother and I visited Paul almost daily in the hospital. It was not an uplifting experience. Some of the sights I witnessed were merely depressing; others scared me into cold sweats. There were men talking to themselves, men digging in the floor for keys, men rocking and chanting to a private choreography. There were men in restraints, housed in rooms down the hall, but I was aware of their presence because of the moaning that wafted from their rooms. There were bars on windows and security everywhere. We always brought Paul his favorite foods and snacks for our visit, trying to show our concern and love, but our time together was often uncomfortable.

Here Paul received medication and was offered the therapy that was needed if he was ever to become a "productive member of society." There was plant therapy, art therapy, music therapy, bullshit therapy. He refused to attend. I never could blame him, though I joined my mother in encouraging participation.

Paul's mental condition stabilized after a few short weeks and he was released. The hospital gave my mother the diagnosis: paranoid schizophrenia. Paul would be "manageable," the hospital said, provided he remained in a controlled environment and took his medication. As if it were that simple.

For a while, Paul complied. But as is common among those who suffer from mental illness, once his mental state appeared to improve and a state of semi-normalcy was restored, Paul decided to self-regulate his medication. Always strong-willed, Paul was determined to stabilize his mental state through the force of that will rather than dependence on medication. Anytime he perceived that we thought he was succumbing to a deeper state of his illness, he would somehow muster the strength to appear normal, even if only for a few hours. But after foregoing his medication for any significant length of time, Paul's delusions intensified.

At first, he couldn't stop smiling. He would sit placidly at the dinner table or in front of the television and, for no apparent reason, break out in fits of laughter. When he wasn't laughing he would glare at others, or me, and just smile. It scared me very much.

Voices and demons lurked in his mind, occupying his every thought, tormenting him day and night. The voices contributed to his obsessive-compulsive disorder. They told him he was ugly and no one wished to look at him, so he would wash and scrub his face for hours on end, until it bled. He would wash and scrub, then retreat to his room, only to reappear ten minutes later to repeat the ritual—never becoming clean or presentable in his own eyes. It was horrible.

Later, the ritual cleansing included his hands. They were washed and washed, scrubbed and brushed until they, too, bled profusely. When asked why he did this so much and so often, Paul replied that they weren't clean yet. During meals, Paul would eat three bites and then excuse himself from the table. Upon his return, it was evident that he had washed his hands. Then he'd take three more bites and excuse himself from the table again. It took forever for him to finish a meal.

After a period of time, the obsessive-compulsive behavior concerning his face and hands ceased; however, he discovered another area of great concern—his teeth. Over and over he would brush them, until his gums bled and were so grossly swollen he couldn't eat. He lost weight at an alarming rate; due in part to not eating because of his gums and in part to the tremendous amount of drugs he was ingesting—drugs that were definitely *not* his prescribed medications.

He would sit in front of the television and internalize every word spoken. He would change the channel and exclaim with wild-eyed excitement that the actors on *that* channel were addressing him, too! Paul would ask a question out loud and then apply whatever was being said on television as an answer to his question.

The voices began to control Paul's world completely, and the last remnants of his sense of reality vanished. He was not only hearing the voices, but conversing with them, openly, as well. Paul rarely left his bedroom unless absolutely necessary, spending hours in solitude. If I listened carefully I could hear him speaking to the voices. Paul was conversing with one of these voices one morning when my mother was out with Phillip, my brother Dan was out, and I was at my father's. As Paul fried bacon for breakfast, the voice asked him if he had a girlfriend. Paul said he didn't. The voice asked if Paul would dare to look at *the voice's* girlfriend if he saw her on the beach. Paul admitted that he would. The voice told Paul that that was improper, and that Paul needed to be punished immediately. The voice commanded Paul to pour hot bacon grease all over his hand. Paul complied. He suffered for weeks from the pain of the burn and the treatment of it, as nurses scrubbed his skin over and over again to avoid infection. Too bad there was no similar treatment for the infection spreading in his mind.

I think Paul recognized, in brief moments of lucidity, that there was a problem. Once, he walked to the local police department and informed them about the voices he heard, telling them how the voices wanted to monopolize various aspects of his life. Whether to mock Paul or in a genuine spirit of compassion for him, the police offered a solution. They outfitted Paul with two AA batteries wrapped in masking tape. He was instructed to keep the contraption with him twenty-four hours a day, except when he took a shower. The police convinced Paul that their device could block any waves that the voices were attempting to transmit to him. When Paul showed the device to my mother and explained what the police had told him, tears filled her eyes.

But Paul believed them, and their theory of the "waves" transmitted by the voices became his new obsession. He spent hours reading encyclopedia after encyclopedia about gamma rays. He wrote page upon page of nonsense and spoke about his ideas with strong conviction. We seldom had company because Paul would dominate every conversation with his bizarre talk about waves and rays. He slept all day and read and wrote all night. I can vividly recall hearing him in the kitchen at two o'clock in the morning—eating, researching, and talking to the voices. I dreaded nighttime and prayed to God that he wouldn't walk down the hall to my room. Oh, how I hoped the voices liked my mother and me.

My mother appealed to Phillip and Dan's sense of filial obligation, asking them to help out by talking to Paul. They made an attempt to explain to Paul that his ideas about gamma rays and voices were distorted and obsessional. But their logical explanations were lost on their younger brother, held as he was in the tight grip of his delusions.

I was often alone with Paul from the time I came home from school until my mother returned from work. My mother asked Paul to stay outside during the day, which made me the gatekeeper if he wanted to come inside the house while I was there—an awkward position, as I was a junior in high school and Paul was twenty-one years old. I was in real fear of being in close proximity to Paul, afraid that he would turn belligerent with me. But I would not—could not—disclose my fears to my mother. She had to go to work, not only for the money, but also for her sanity.

Paul didn't have many friends, and the few he did have couldn't be considered a positive influence. Paul's cronies would assemble in our front yard in the afternoon, to nod as Paul related his latest findings about the supernatural. The more drugs they ingested, the more raptly they listened to Paul's ravings.

Claudia M. Jones, Ph.D.

Sometimes I peered out my window to watch the ritual. They would fill a tall drinking glass with pot or hash, light it, and turn the glass upside-down on top of an album jacket. Then they'd slide the glass to the end of the album jacket and inhale as much smoke as they could. They became high within seconds, while others in the group stood by smoking joints or popping pills as they waited their turn. Watching this, I resolved I would never touch a drug in my life, and I never have.

My mother gave Paul his prescribed medications daily, but he put them in a box in his room. We found the box one day, its contents overflowing. But Paul's desire for any kind of drug except the medications which could have helped him was insatiable, and drove him to steal anything he could lay his hands on. Some items reappeared eventually, others will never be found. Once, we were all standing in the kitchen when my mother exclaimed that her silver tea set, gold tea set, and other elegant pieces were missing from her two china cabinets. Some of the missing pieces actually belonged to Dan, and the idea that Paul would steal even from him infuriated Dan beyond words.

I lost count of how many times Paul was taken away under the Baker Act.[1] Each brief hiatus supposedly stabilized Paul and he was released within days. Sometimes we were fortunate and he was incarcerated for a few weeks so that we could rejuvenate ourselves. Upon each return home, Paul promised to take his medication, but such promises were never kept. Life seemed to move at an extremely rapid pace during this time. I wanted to savor the special moments from my last two years of high school, but as Paul continued to struggle, a part of me wanted to wish the time away so that I could find out how the saga would end.

I was quite active in high school and enjoyed my friends and the various activities we participated in. I looked forward to my junior year homecoming football game, knowing it would be a memorable event. It certainly was, but not in the way that I anticipated. During the day of the big game, the cheerleaders

---

[1] The Baker Act is a Florida law which allows a physician or law enforcement personnel to take an individual deemed dangerous to himself or others to a hospital or crisis center against his will, where he or she must be evaluated within seventy-two hours. Following the evaluation, if the individual is not released and does not agree to voluntary treatment, the hospital or crisis center can petition the court to have the individual confined for treatment involuntarily.

attended the all-boys parochial high school pep rally. We cheered and anticipated an exciting football game and sock hop afterwards. When the pep rally ended, I went to my girlfriend's house, where my mother was to pick us up on her way home from work, feed us, and drop us off at the game.

When we pulled up to our house, I noticed that the front curtains were drawn—the first indication that a problem existed inside. When my mother unlocked the front door there was nothing but darkness, everywhere. I felt bile rise to my throat when she flicked on the light. There was a hole in the ceiling approximately six feet in diameter, and plaster was everywhere. We walked through the house in silence, finding a similar hole in the ceiling of every room. If I felt faint, I can't imagine how my mother felt. Her face was as white as the piles of plaster that filled the house. We knew, of course, that Paul was responsible, but why had he done it? My girlfriend escorted me to my bedroom and told me to be strong for my mother's sake. My mother had gone to comfort Paul, who was sitting in the darkness of his bedroom.

He had heard voices coming out of the air vent in his room. He'd left his room, but couldn't escape the voices—they had followed him and spoken to him via every air vent throughout the house. My resourceful brother had called a taxi, instructing the driver to pick up several insect bombs and deliver them to the house. He had no money, and I have no idea what he gave as payment. He had then opened up the air vents and slid the poison inside, in the hope that it would stop the voices. He'd returned to his room and lain on his bed, waiting for the poison to work. He had imagined a rifle pointed at him from the air vent. This had been more than he could stand. He had had enough. He'd retrieved a baseball bat from the garage and had smashed ten six-foot holes in various rooms of our house in his efforts to destroy the rifle.

After calling my father and brothers to come deal with the mess, my mother came to my room and announced that my friend and I were *not* going to miss our senior year homecoming game and sock hop. She left the chaos and dropped us off at the game, just in time to see the opening kick-off. I was grateful once again for my mother's remarkable strength. My friend never mentioned it again.

Claudia M. Jones, Ph.D.

The hospital record of Paul's involuntary admission following this incident is reproduced here verbatim:

> This is the first psychiatric admission for this 21-year-old patient, brought by the police to the hospital under the Baker Act. The reason was that his family called the police after they found out that the patient was making big holes in the ceiling to find the body of a dead man, supposedly lying up there while being guarded by a gunman looking down at patient. The patient was very paranoiac, and he was thinking that everybody in his family was a communist. He refused his physical, claiming that nobody is to touch him, or should touch him, and lab findings CBC, SMA-12, and urinalysis for drug screening were negative.
>
> <u>Problem #1</u> - Delusional thinking.
>
> For the last couple of weeks, the patient was very delusional, thinking that he would be able to invent a machine that would be good to screen people, and to read the peoples' minds, and at the same time he was afraid that the same machine would see inside his brain. His behavior during the hospital stay was very withdrawn, very defensive. He was not participating in the group, and he was not going to sign a voluntary admission. For this reason, a court hearing was necessary. The patient as I said was very uncooperative, was not participating in group therapy, and he was completely on the defense because he was refusing to be touched. He didn't refuse his medication, which was Thorazine 300mg PO tid, and he was not in restraints, but was confined to his pajamas for close observation. After the hearing, the patient became more aware of his thinking and realizing there was no dead body with a gunman in the ceiling and being forced to stay one more week in the hospital, he started giving more participation... giving more cooperation with the staff to the point that the precautions were removed and he was going to apply for Group Level II.

> *Problem Level #2 – This was again expressed by seeing the dead body and gunman. The dead hallucinations stopped as soon as his brother told him that there was no body in the ceiling. The patient was on continuous medication, appeared less anxious, and less scared. Still, some of his thoughts are paranoid type, still thinking that some forces are controlling his thinking. Because of the judge's orders, we are going to discharge him tomorrow with follow up at Davis Memorial Hospital. He will have a month's supply of medication, just Thorazine, which he has been taking also in the past. He is physically well. He is competent for VA purposes. He can go back to work for a part-time job, since he has been involved in work whether he would start going to 12 hours or more. He is non-convalescent, and his prognosis is very guarded.*

As the hospital record indicates, Paul had a fixation with death and, once discharged and back home, left obvious clues for us to find. The yellow pages were left opened to the gun section. A noose was found hanging in the garage. When confronted about his actions, Paul just smiled. But the voices, the delusions, the paranoia, and the blinding headaches Paul was now experiencing were too much for him to bear, and he decided that he had to leave this world. After much thought about how best to accomplish this, Paul injected Black Flag insecticide into his forearm, hoping that the poison would engulf his body. It didn't, in fact, kill him, but he was terribly sick. We had to resort to the Baker Act once more and off to the hospital he went, only to be once more stabilized and released.

One night in June 1981, I was on the phone in my mother's room when Paul staggered in. He was weaving back and forth and seemed barely able to stand. His shorts were cut at the crotch and he wore no underwear, so that he was fully exposed. I hung up the phone and tried to ask Paul what was wrong, only I couldn't see the whites of his eyes. I followed him, my heart beating wildly, as he staggered into the kitchen and tried to make a phone call. He pulled on the telephone cord in an attempt regain his balance, then fell straight back onto the terrazzo floor. I ran to get help from Dan, who called the ambulance to transport Paul to the hospital and called my mother, who was at church, practicing singing for my cousin's wedding, to tell her what had happened.

At the hospital, Paul was placed in a freezing room with his hands and feet strapped down. A plastic apparatus was inserted in his mouth and down his throat, to keep him from biting his tongue. Periodically, his body shook violently as he tried to writhe free of the restraints. His stomach was pumped and then he was left, strapped down, to throw up on his own. He couldn't be left alone, but my mother and brothers had to work. I held a vigil over my twenty-two-year-old brother, standing by with buckets and towels while he fought for his life. Countless times he opened his eyes, but couldn't focus well enough to recognize my familiar face. I was so frightened that at one point I joined Paul in throwing up all over the floor.

Once Paul was purged of the poisons in his system, he was moved to a private room. My mother arrived after work and our priest, a family friend, joined her later. When Paul was able to speak so that he made sense, my mother asked what happened. We learned that Paul had purchased fifty Quaaludes, given four away, and swallowed the remaining forty-six in an attempt to end his life. In front of the priest, Paul confessed that he thought life would be much better for my mother if he were dead. I asked why he'd worn shorts cut at the crotch and no underwear. He said he'd thought it would be the easiest thing for the undertaker to remove. The pain for all of us, hearing that, was excruciating. My mother was truly heartbroken. Even after all she had endured with Paul, he was still her Pomato Boy. Unable to offer him a better remedy, she still offered her unconditional love.

The same could not be said of others in our immediate and extended family. Phillip and Dan wanted nothing to do with Paul, and my mother often asked me not to tell my brothers about various incidents. Whenever they did become involved, they would enter the scene ex post facto, clearly disapproving of whatever course of action my mother had taken but offering no solutions, only their opinions of "You should have done this" and "I certainly wouldn't have done that."

Grandparents, aunts, uncles, and cousins might ask, "How are you, Paul?" but didn't want to hear, or know, the real answer. Paul had always greatly enjoyed family gatherings and parties; he often assisted my mother with the preparations, and his enthusiasm and energy were incredibly high as he vacuumed the house, singing his favorite tunes. But more and more frequently, once the hour of the festivities arrived Paul retreated to the sanctuary of his bedroom, unhappy at being excluded socially. Some relatives made the polite gesture of giving him gifts at birthdays and holidays, while denying him the things that to Paul would truly have been gifts—a genuine interest in his life, a real conversation, a sign of affection.

Often my mother would be invited to parties, celebrations, or dinners for which no invitation was extended to Paul. But she wouldn't go if Paul wasn't included, and did her best to shield him from the unpleasant truth. If he noticed that it was Memorial Day and asked if Uncle Chris was having his annual barbecue, she would tell him, although it pained her deeply to lie, "No honey, it's just his immediate family this year." Invariably she would add, "But let's you and I do something instead," and they would shop for something special to cook at home or dress up and go to a restaurant. Paul was content in my mother's companionship, and my mother, although she missed many social events, was content in knowing that Paul was treated with love and respect.

My mother never scolded Paul, never belittled him, and never stopped loving him and hoping for an answer. This was no easy feat even when Paul was at his best. For anyone less compassionate than my mother, it would have been nearly impossible when Paul's belligerence was directed, as it sometimes was, toward her. My mother was busy in the kitchen one evening as I sat at the counter, talking to her. Paul wanted cigarettes, which my mother had resorted to rationing to him; left to his own devices, Paul would chain-smoke pack after pack. He had some change, but was fifty cents short of what he needed to buy cigarettes. He nagged at my mother, nonstop, to give him the fifty cents. He claimed that he had a terrible headache and needed a cigarette. She refused. He persisted, and became quite livid as each request was denied.

My mother is 4'11" and very petite. Paul is 5'11", and because he walks everywhere, for miles a day, he's very lean and strong—and entirely capable of inflicting serious harm in a physical altercation. Yet, when he towered over her and yelled that his head was hurting him, she still calmly refused to give him the fifty cents. Paul reacted by cornering her against the kitchen cabinets and taking her tiny neck in his left hand. With his right hand he pointed a large carving knife at her face. "Are you going to give me the fifty cents or am I going to have to kill you?" She relented and gave him the money, and he left, nonchalantly, for the store.

I was frightened and furious, and asked her to please call the police, to please do something, anything. Her response shocked me. She said, "Can you imagine how terrible his headaches must be for him to act that way?"

My mother never excused or justified Paul's behavior—nor did she ask any of us to do so. She did, however, accept Paul and his actions, and she taught us to do the same. Paul was Paul. There was no place for self-pity in our lives. And although sometimes I felt it would have been soothing to confide in someone outside the situation the great amount of frustration I felt, it was expected that, to the extent possible, what happened in our home was to remain private.

This became less and less possible as Paul's illness escalated. He was arrested numerous times, on charges ranging from drug possession to theft to assault on a police officer, but was never convicted. Each time we noticed something stolen, the police were called in, and Paul was arrested and taken to the local jail to be held. Sometimes he was there for weeks, sometimes for months—time which gave us a much-needed respite during which to regroup and regain our sanity.

Eventually Paul's behavior made it obvious to everyone, even complete strangers, that something was wrong. Once when my mother took Paul to Burger King for a meal, a man sat eating at a table next to them, minding his own business. Paul imagined that the man was staring at them and mocking him. He calmly got up, walked over to the gentleman, asked what he was looking at, and spit on his food. He then walked out and waited for my mother at her car. She was left to pick up the pieces of yet another mess created by Paul. She apologized profusely to the man, who asked, "He's sick, isn't he?" My poor mother just nodded.

Perhaps Paul's ultimate public spectacles were the letter he wrote to President Reagan in the summer of 1981, propounding his ideas about brain waves and a machine that could read people's minds, and the Record of Invention form he filed with the

U.S. Patent office about this invention, which he alternately referred to as "Diode" or "The Machine."

(Letter to President Reagan)

August 28, 1981

To Whom it May Concern,

I believe I have discovered something that may help this country. It started three years ago when I became interested in nuclear chemistry. I believe a lot of people have ESP wheater they know it or not, so I thought it would be great if we had a machine that could tap in on people's minds! So I started thinking, what makes the mind tick? My answer, brain waves, and radium causes brain waves. Alpha, Beta, and Gamma. Alpha I believe is your conversational thoughts and Gamma being your innermost thoughts, and Beta being your dream thoughts. It goes something like this; Radium creates Gamma Waves and Pitchblende creates, or Uranite with is a crystalized form, which is better than bromide to use, Beta and Alpha Waves.

If a radar gun was to be pointted at someone, or something like a radar gun, it would cause them to be radioactive, but not harmful. And say a mile or better, or any distance desired, there is a converted radar machine which is attached to a TV set or several. The radar machine sends out the chemicals which are in the dial in the TV set. The dial must be made out of bismuth, because when polonain which comes from Uranite, bombards with bismuth it is called the only natural accuring fission. Somewhere in the TV set there is a betatron, maybe not. Whatever the person see's shows up on the TV scene, and there are three recorder's, one for each brain wave. If a bismuth room is made around it you should be able to talk in the person's mind. Then there should be one recorder that can take words of

Claudia M. Jones, Ph.D.

one recorder and place it on the main one. I thank you kindly.

Sincerely Yours,
Paul G. Maurer

P.S. Please answer

SKETCH OF INVENTION

IN THE SPACE BELOW, MAKE A SKETCH OF YOUR INVENTION. (IF YOU ALREADY HAVE SKETCHES OR PHOTOGRAPHS, THEY WILL SERVE THE PURPOSE AND MAY BE ATTACHED TO THIS SHEET.) THE SKETCH YOU MAKE NEED NOT BE A FINISHED DRAWING; SIMPLY ENOUGH TO ENABLE US TO UNDERSTAND YOUR INVENTION.

Diode

① T.V. Set - First Step To The "Machine"

Any Thing the person sees it appears on the T/ set in color!

PICTURE

Di oDe

GAMMA SPECHER — BETA SPECHER

② RaDar Machine is connected to the T.V. - It sends the chemicals out to the persons mind

① Pitchblende or uranite which is a crystalized form, uranium and radium are placed inside the Bismuth "Diode" and when neutrons bombard Bismuth therefore uranium and at the same time picks up the other chemicals

③ Alpha speacher "conversation thoughts" picks up all Alpha rays or waves — Beta speacher picks up all Beta rays or waves there called Dream Thoughts — Gama speacher picks up all Gama rays or waves called Innermost Thought

T.V.

Radar Gun

A radar gun is pointed at someone and then picks the chemical the Radar Machine has sent out then sends the rays or wave back to the T.V.!

As nonsensical as Paul's "Sketch of Invention" appears, even more puzzling may be the reply he received from the managing director of Washington Patent Office Searches:

> *July 20, 1982*
>
> *Re: Maurer — DIODE*
>
> *Dear Mr. Maurer:*
>
> *We acknowledge receipt of the Record of Invention form containing a complete disclosure of your above identified invention.*
>
> *We have carefully analyzed your disclosure and find the same sufficiently complete for an immediate preliminary patentability search.*
>
> *If the preliminary patentability search report is favorable, as regards the novelty of your invention, it is our opinion that your invention would appear to possess definite commercial merit.*
>
> *Therefore, upon receiving the search fee of $150.00, we will proceed immediately with the patentability search, which is the first step in the protection and commercialization of your invention.*
>
> *Sincerely yours,*
> *Washington Patent Office Searches*

Other than providing them with the $150 search fee, it's difficult to imagine what "definite commercial merit" the agency found in Paul's sketch of a machine he claimed could broadcast a person's thoughts onto a television screen—in color, as he noted.

*****

I graduated from high school in 1981 and in the fall of that year entered a parochial university to study education. My mother was elated for me. She wanted me to have a taste of campus life, so although we lived only thirty minutes from the university, I lived in the dorms. In retrospect, it was a wonderful gesture on my mother's part, but at the time I missed her terribly. We were, and still are, the closest of friends.

My father, however, who never acknowledged or involved himself in Paul's problems, now had serious problems of his own. After smoking three packs of cigarettes a day for many years, my father was diagnosed with throat cancer—an ironic turn of events for a speech pathologist. The doctors performed a tracheotomy, and my father began, perhaps, to understand some of the mental and physical torment his son had already endured for years. What is a runner without legs? Or a pianist with no hands? What is a speech pathologist with no voice? It was difficult for my father to accept such a fate, and he began to crumble. He drank more than ever in an attempt to ease the pain. He sat on the couch and just stared out the window, beside him a shot glass of whiskey and a beer.

I worked as a compensatory education teacher for a kindergarten class in 1982 and 1983. Coincidentally, my father worked as a speech pathologist in a diagnostic center in the building adjacent to the one in which I worked. We saw one another daily, during which time I saw my father's health deteriorate at an alarming rate. Whenever he coughed, he held his arms close to his sides because the pain was terrible. A visit to the doctor revealed a one-and-a-half-inch mark on his lung. An operation was scheduled for the day after Father's Day.

On Father's Day he was in wonderful spirits, displaying no fear whatsoever. One of his brothers was there, and tales of the good ol' days were shared. My father said he would be fine and nothing was going to get him down... he was ready to fight for me, his Buttercup. It was an awkward Father's Day, but a moving one as well.

At first I was told that the operation went quite well—that the doctors removed half a lung, and that my father would need chemotherapy and radiation for a while. The truth, however, was revealed to me by my mother days later. When the doctors had opened up my father, they found his entire body, including his lymph nodes, infested with cancer. They closed him right back up. The doctors and my uncles decided to lie to my father about his condition, assuming that he would give up the fight if he knew the truth. Knowing my father, they made a good call.

I went to visit my father in the hospital after the operation. A nurse passed by pushing a wheelchair, and I moved out of the way, saying "excuse me" because I was blocking her turn. In the wheelchair was a shriveled man with sunken eyes, who stared at me. I nodded, although I didn't recognize him. When the nurse wheeled him into his room, I raced to the nurse's station to inquire who he was, dreading the answer that she gave me: Dr. Maurer, my father. The nurse asked how long it had been since I'd last seen him. It had been only four days.

My father was still under the assumption he'd had half a lung removed and required a little chemotherapy. Because he couldn't drive and everyone else worked, I transported him to and from his chemotherapy. The frail man would sit in the front seat of my car with a bucket between his legs because he got violently sick during the entire ride home. He was weak, often too weak to talk. Once he jotted a short note apologizing for not socializing with me, but the chemotherapy was taking its toll on him. I would put him to bed and remain for the day to ensure he had everything he needed, including some company. This routine went on for the whole of the long summer.

My brother Phillip was married in November 1983. Dan and I were both in the wedding, but Paul was in jail and Phillip did not extend an invitation to my father.

My father and I had planned that I would visit him the day before Thanksgiving, after my classes at the university were finished. I had to return his camera, which I'd borrowed and which he wanted for Thanksgiving Day. But my plans changed, and I phoned my father to let him know that I was going out with college friends that Wednesday night and would see him on Thanksgiving with his camera. He understood.

No one else was home when I returned that night after seeing my friends—my mother was at choir rehearsal, Phillip was at his own home, Dan was working on a presentation, and Paul was in jail. The phone rang; when I answered, my father's wife told me that she'd come home from work and found my father on the floor, dead.

It seems that my father knew he was dying. He'd kept an hourly account of the day's events, beginning with his morning trip to McDonald's. By noon, he'd recorded impaired vision and a swollen tongue, and a decision to take no more medication. At four o'clock he'd noted that, having worked with stroke victims, he recognized he was dying. He wrote the words to Frank Sinatra's "My Way," and that was the end. The coroner determined the cause of death to be heart failure—an ironic end for a man who so often seemed heartless. In light of all that my father had done and not done, it now seems strange that I mourned his passing at all. But he was still my father, and I was his Buttercup, and at his funeral I cried to think that if I'd been with him the afternoon that he'd died, as we'd originally planned, maybe I could have done something.

My father had the last word, as always. In addition to leaving nothing—not a penny or a single possession—to any of us, he was so bitter about his estrangement from Phillip that he excluded his firstborn entirely from his obituary. It didn't matter to Phillip in the least, but it did to me. What could I answer when people asked, "Why did your father only mention two sons?" To the last, I wished I understood what went through the man's disturbed mind.

My mother had to deliver the news to Paul in jail. As soon as he saw my mother he said, "Dad's dead, isn't he?" She nodded. And in spite of everything, Paul put his face in his hands and wept.

*****

From jail, Paul was eventually transferred to the forensics unit at Florida State Hospital at Chattahoochee, where he spent three long years in an attempt at rehabilitation. I visited him there as often as possible and brought him food and clothes when he needed them, as well as other things he sometimes requested. He mentioned wanting a radio, which I delivered—only to be told upon my next visit that he'd sold it for cigarettes within minutes of my departure. At another visit, Paul admired my religious medallion and chain. Without a moment's thought, I put them around his neck. Both were gifts to me, but I wanted him to have them, to leave him with a feeling of family. I later learned that they, too, had been sold—for goodies at the commissary. Generally our visits were good, though, and I nodded along with him at his ideas and dreams for his life upon his release. My heart ached for what had become of my brother, and I, too, dreamed that he might have a better, more productive life.

But that was not to be the case. Within a year and a half of being released from Chattahoochee, Paul was involuntarily placed in another mental hospital, this time at Pembroke Pines, which at least had the advantage of being near my home, making it easier for me to visit Paul and possible for him to visit me occasionally. During his time there, Paul held something of a leadership position among the patients. He circulated a petition to have various changes implemented throughout his unit, related to the lack of proper treatment given to those with whom he shared a common fate. In particular, Paul was troubled about the care of one man who was under physical restraint—literally shackled to his bed—constantly. Paul volunteered to feed the man all three meals each day, perceiving that having this task performed by a fellow inmate rather than by staff would restore to the man some small degree of dignity.

At the hospital Paul had to earn each privilege, from having a cigarette to wearing street clothes rather than a uniform. When a 24-hour weekend pass was earned, it was decided that Paul would stay with me; I lived closer to the hospital, and the unstructured environment of my mother's house allowed too many temptations for Paul to fall into old habits. I would pick him up and sign all the necessary paperwork with the administrative staff, who were enclosed in a caged office. The television would be blaring and rows of Paul's compatriots sat staring placidly at whatever was on the screen. Others walked through the fog of cigarette smoke, not knowing where they were headed. During the sign-out process, I would notice the many sad eyes watching Paul, longing to be in his shoes. The stench of those surroundings followed Paul to my home, permeating the clothes he wore as well as the clothes in the laundry bag he brought with him to be washed.

Before his visits, Paul would call me over and over to reaffirm that he was still coming. Almost as soon as he arrived, he would begin to worry about being late getting back to the facility. He would call the "correct time" phone number, then within seconds of hanging up would call again. Very early one morning while Paul was visiting, I heard the phone next to the bed sounding off the seven-digit phone number Paul was dialing on the phone in the kitchen. After hearing this for the seventh time in a matter of minutes, I went to the kitchen and asked Paul what the hell he was doing. "Oh, I'm sorry," he said, looking like a scolded child. "I just don't want to be late." I assured him that I would have him back on time.

Paul was obsessed with not only the time but also the date. He'd once told my mother that if anyone found out that he didn't know the day, month, and year, he could be locked away. Occasionally he would blurt out, "Today's Sunday the fifteenth of March, 1987, right?" And we would assure him that he was in the right place at the right time.

For many years following his release from the mental hospital, Paul never showed any signs of improvement. He never received any more therapy and usually declined his medication. When possible, my mother exerted control and explained to Paul that he couldn't stay in the house unless he took his Prolixin shot, which he hated because the Prolixin caused his left hand to ball up and twitch uncontrollably and constantly.

At one point in the late 1980s, the government referred Paul to a community housing development in which he would be given his own apartment with a roommate. A middle-aged husband and wife team ran the establishment and distributed medication to an apartment building full of individuals with assorted special needs. The living conditions were dirty and unsanitary, yet Paul moved in and tried to make it work. When my mother and I bought some things to decorate his dilapidated room, our hearts sank. It was far worse than any hospital—mattresses with holes, broken and hanging cabinet doors, cigarette burns in the carpet, holes and cracks in the peeling plastered walls, and the inevitable stench that seemed to accompany mental illness. But Paul, as always, uncomplainingly accepted the situation in which he found himself. He unpacked the groceries we'd brought and tried to settle in. Even as we returned to the car, I think we knew it would never last. Paul couldn't thrive in an environment so unlike the home he knew.

Paul's roommate was an extremely elderly gentleman who had no legs. One day, not knowing his roommate was an alcoholic, Paul wheeled him to a local bar where they spent hours drinking and talking with each other. The administration was not pleased and shortly thereafter, Paul moved back home.

As he became more secluded due to his aberrant behavior, his social skills deteriorated. To bring a friend home was often embarrassing and uncomfortable. Paul would try to hold a conversation, but talked—confusedly and ceaselessly—about the most inappropriate topics. Eventually, people stopped coming over. One person, though, had seemingly endless patience with and understanding of Paul—Brian, the man I was to marry on February 4, 1989.

Paul was an usher in our wedding and proudly walked my mother down the aisle. He was somehow able to hold it together for our special day, dancing and socializing to the best of his ability. When he wasn't dancing or eating, Paul was busy helping out. He cleared plates, took drink orders, and asked many of the more than one hundred guests if there was anything they needed or any way he could be of assistance. My father-in-law took note of Paul's pleasure at being of service and later commented on what a hard and willing worker he is.

But in his day-to-day life, social interaction was not easy for Paul. Every so often, he would try to make "friends" with someone he'd met, by trying to impress them as being a big spender. In order to get the money to do so, he continued to steal from the family. Paul took televisions, radios, cameras, whatever he could get his hands on. Sometimes he would give away our food, and other times he returned groceries and bought drugs and alcohol with the refunded money. He even stole from my jewelry box the one possession of my father's that any of us had. Although my father himself had left us nothing, his second wife had given his Fordham University ring to Dan, who didn't want it and gave it to me. Paul discovered the ring in my jewelry box and sold it for drugs. It was sad, yet typical of Paul's capriciousness, that he could weep over the loss of a father who'd never been one, then discard our only material remembrance of him to buy drugs.

Paul was fixated on my father, his death, and the fact that he'd left Paul nothing. My mother even gave Paul bus money so he could go downtown to the courthouse and view the will for himself. He couldn't accept it; he thought my mother had the money left to him by my father and was hiding it. He disappeared for several days, and when he returned, demanding that my mother hand over the money from my father's will, she was afraid of him. She wouldn't let him in the house, but communicated with him through a tiny window in the door. They argued at length until my mother realized it was pointless. She told Paul that she would give him a check.

When she turned to go to her room, Paul broke through the front door. He grabbed my mother by the nape of her neck and rammed her head repeatedly on the desk. Rage which had built up over a lifetime of hurt, frustration, and mental illness mixed with the crack he'd smoked in a deadly combination. Paul was completely out of control and my mother was helpless.

When he finished beating her, he asked her for cigarettes. He went into the kitchen to make a sandwich, but first called the police to alert them of his actions. As my mother staggered toward her bedroom she saw the hole Paul had made in the front door and crawled through it to the safety of our neighbor's house.

By the time the police arrived, Paul had eaten his sandwich. On the way to the police car he turned to my mother, who watched from the neighbor's lawn, and said, "You see that, bitch? The next time I'm gonna kill you." Paul was taken to jail and my mother was taken to the hospital.

I was five months pregnant with my first child when Dan called to tell me what had happened. My mother had been stitched up and discharged from the hospital, so I raced to her house. I was shocked at how badly she'd been beaten. I brushed her hair to soothe her, and also because she was unable to raise her arms to do it herself. Hair came out in clumps with each stroke, and I watched in disbelief as it fell to the floor.

I walked through my mother's house amidst toppled furniture and bloodstained carpets. On the kitchen counter was the opened jar of mayonnaise that Paul had used to make his sandwich. There was blood, his mixed with hers, all over the counter top and inside the jar. To this day, I cannot eat mayonnaise.

Later we received a phone call from the police department, asking my mother to fill out the necessary paperwork. I accompanied her to the station and watched as she painstakingly wrote a complete account of what had transpired the night before. My mother later dropped her charges of assault and battery, but due to the severity of the crime, the state prosecuted Paul. He was taken to jail in February 1990, and because his case went back and forth in court due to the question of his competency and mental state at the time of the crime, he remained there for nearly two years. We didn't hear from him for quite a long while. He never made any attempt to contact the family—not for clothes, cigarettes, money, or visits.

My first child, Anastasia, was born later that year, on June 24, 1990. A new baby is a joyous event in any family and in ours especially, after everything we'd been through in the past few years. Anastasia had a positive effect on everyone, especially my mother. I tried to spend as much time as I could at my mother's house. We were there when Paul phoned late at night on Christmas Eve. I was amazed to hear his voice, but all I could say to him was, "Why did you do it?" to which he answered, "I don't know."

My mother and I visited Paul for the first time since he'd been convicted of assaulting her. It was a familiar routine for us, as we had visited him countless times before in the psychiatric ward or in jail. But it had been a long time, and I had forgotten how much I hated the smell of these institutions.

Paul was behind a glass wall, but we seemed to have more than the usual difficulty understanding what he was saying—until we realized his jaw had been broken and was wired shut. Evidently, he'd been tapping on the table in his jail cell, which annoyed another inmate. A fight had ensued and Paul had lost. Communication was nearly impossible, and Paul pounded on the glass, trying to make us understand him. We couldn't. He was by turns bitterly angry, then merely tired and confused. He looked like a lost soul. Our inability to decode his mumbling only increased his frustration, and as the tension intensified we decided it was time for us to go. As we walked away, I could hear his fist pounding against the glass. I drove my mother home and watched her wipe away more tears. I wondered how much longer this could go on.

CHAPTER 4
FAITH AND HOPE

But life did go on. I entered a Ph.D. program in the fall of 1991, which pleased my mother and the rest of my family. When we were able to have contact visits with Paul, he would boast to the guard, "This is my sister. She's going to be a doctor." I'm not sure whether he understood that I wasn't going to be an M.D., but rather a doctor of philosophy specializing in education.

Paul was released from jail in the summer of 1992. I was pregnant with my second child. My mother helped him rent an apartment and even took him to purchase a car. Paul was happy to be free and thrilled with the independence of having his own apartment and car. Things seemed, finally, to be going well for Paul. But entropy rules, and on August 24, 1992, Hurricane Andrew demolished much of South Florida, including Paul's fragile new independence.

During the hurricane I hid with my husband, mother, two-year-old Anastasia and newborn Karyn, who was only eight days old, in a utility closet for hours. It was a frightening experience, and the destruction left in the hurricane's wake was overwhelming. Paul's apartment was completely ruined, and he didn't know how to cope. Although Paul was adept at *causing* chaos, he didn't handle it well when it was inflicted upon him. There were plenty of jobs to be found as South Florida worked to recover from the storm damage, but rather than stay and earn money during the recovery effort, Paul left.

He ended up in South Carolina, where he found work and seemed to be happy. I think my mother was glad of the peace and quiet she enjoyed when Paul was away, so she helped him financially to the extent that she was able. Even so, Paul would often have no food, no place to stay, and no money. Whenever this happened, he would find the closest hospital and check himself in. Paul knows the system, and the system knows Paul. In spite of his many shortcomings, Paul is a survivor. His physical toughness is equally matched by his mental toughness, and he has never complained about the conditions of his life.

My third child, Brian, was born on April 21, 1995, while Paul was still in South Carolina. He returned home that fall, however, and was able to attend my Ph.D. graduation party in December. I was asked to read at my graduation Mass the evening prior to commencement, which I considered a tremendous honor. Unfortunately, my husband babysat our three children and my mother couldn't attend because it would mean that Paul would be left outside for too long. Phillip and Dan weren't interested, so I experienced this once-in-a-lifetime honor alone.

My family was able to join in the celebration two weeks later, though, at my graduation party. One hundred friends were in attendance, a few of whom spoke on my behalf. I was in my glory, listening to a close friend recall our Ph.D. classes together, when Paul stood up and began to question the speaker, making no sense. I was embarrassed and humiliated beyond words, wishing someone would just shut him up. But no one did, and so the bizarre exchange of words continued until Paul was satisfied. He sat down, pleased with himself, and I drank. Why had I thought this special night would be spared? It was inevitable that Paul would ruin it.

Although more often frightening or mortifying, like the graduation party scene, some of the incidents which were an inherent part of life with Paul were actually rather funny. He has a wonderful sense of humor and enjoys telling stories and joking with anyone who will listen. Some of Paul's humor was unintentional, resulting from the complete honesty that prompted him to say whatever was on his mind, such as the time he remarked, "Hey Claudia, you cut your hair." I was surprised he noticed, and so I asked, "Do you like it?" He responded, "No, not really. You look like Twiggy."

Paul often accompanied my mother to our house for Sunday night dinner. It was a special family time that usually went well. Often they would come early enough in the afternoon that Paul could help Brian with the lawn or other projects around the house. One afternoon, in an effort to boost Paul's confidence, Brian gave him some clippers. What a mistake! Our trees, bushes, and shrubs were barely recognizable after the thorough trimming Paul gave them. He wiped out years of growth in a matter of minutes. Brian freaked out as my mother and I tried to contain our laughter. Our neighbors, too, were quite amused. After his initial shock, even Brian was able to laugh about it, but, needless to say, yard work was stricken from the list of Paul's chores around our house.

He remains, though, the first person Brian calls for assistance when there is manual labor to be done. Since Paul has no car and has sold every bicycle he's ever owned, he is forced to walk everywhere he wants to go. As a result, he is quite lean and strong, and is capable of accomplishing any task requiring physical strength with ease. Whenever Paul visits to help Brian work, the two go out afterwards for a meal, a beer, a few games of pool, cigars—a chance to socialize as any two men might do after a day's work. Brian has always paid Paul for his work, although the money is usually spent by the next day. But, as Brian says, Paul is a man and should be treated as one.

For several years after the landscaping debacle, Paul continued to live as a transient, shuttling between Florida and South Carolina with periodic hospitalizations—some voluntary, some involuntary. My mother called me one day from work saying she was afraid of Paul, so Brian and I worked with law enforcement to hospitalize him yet again under the Baker Act. We spent hours in a downtown office completing mounds of paperwork. Then we met plainclothes officers near my mother's house to identify Paul for them. He was walking the streets, disheveled and unkempt, barefoot and talking to himself. When one of the cars approached him, he spit in an officer's face. As a result, when they reached the local hospital Paul was heavily medicated and put in hand and foot restraints for twenty-four hours, which intensified his frustration. Later, when he was finally taken to his room, he appeared calm. But on the way to the cafeteria he darted out the doors and walked over twenty-five miles, in bare feet, to hide at my grandmother's vacant house.

I'd specifically forewarned both the officers and hospital of Paul's particular aversion to restraints, and had asked them to please handle him with extreme care. When I learned what had happened at the hospital, I felt sick, fearing that Paul would feel I'd betrayed him. Thankfully, although much to my surprise, Paul was not angry for what Brian and I had done on behalf of my mother. I believe that on some level he understood that it was necessary.

It was and will always be important to me that Paul know me as an ally; I didn't want him to ever shut me out as he had everyone else. Our rapport, however tenuous, is important to both of us. One of my most precious possessions is a charm that Paul gave me years ago after a heated argument in which I lost my temper with him and he responded in kind, frightening me badly. A few days later, Paul presented me with the charm, which is shaped like a stop sign and is inscribed *I'll never stop loving you.* That tender gesture, from someone many would believe incapable of tenderness, is one of my most cherished memories, and I've never worn the charm for fear of losing it.

When we learned that I was pregnant with twins, our house immediately went up for sale (the landscaping had grown back by then!) as we knew we'd need a larger one, and we had to move to an apartment for a time. Paul and my mother came one Sunday for our family dinner, but encountered some difficulty with the code at the apartment's front gate. My mother stayed in the car at the gate, but Paul, infuriated, walked through the pouring rain up to the apartment, using the most foul language I have ever heard. Brian asked him to leave and he did, but certainly not quietly. He cursed and yelled obscene racial remarks, causing a tremendous scene for all our new neighbors to behold. I had always said that Paul was welcome in our home as long as he behaved. But because my children were old enough to understand the terrible things Paul shouted, I refused to allow him in my house again until he could control his behavior. It pained me deeply to close our door to him, but I vowed that my children would not become involved in this mess. That day was the last time I would see Paul for almost two years.

He returned to South Carolina, and we spoke on the phone when he would call to ask me to send him a care package. At one point the phone calls stopped, and my mother became worried. I phoned various hospitals, but Paul wasn't at any of them. I contacted the jail and learned that he had been picked up on a six-year-old bench warrant. When he was released in January 2001, after spending only a week or two in jail until the matter of the outstanding bench warrant was resolved, he came to see my mother and I visited him at her house. It was the first time he saw the twins, Patrick and Joseph, one of whom has "Paul" as his middle name. At forty-two, Paul looked like an old man and seemed tired—tired of fighting, tired of life, tired of *his* life.

For the last few years, Paul has continued to move back and forth between our hometown and South Carolina. He works at various odd jobs when he can get them, and walks away the hours of his long, lonely days when there is no work to occupy his time. He is calmer now and better able to control his behavior, so whenever he is here, my door is once again open to this worn man. We listen to his tales, dreams, and ideas of grandeur with smiles and nods of encouragement. My children idolize him, which makes him feel quite important. Although we continue to hope, we've all resigned ourselves to the fact that probably nothing will change for Paul. And no medication, no doctor, no therapy can ever restore to my brother what was taken from him by mental illness—the chance of a normal life.

In June 2002, Paul was in South Carolina when he once again encountered trouble with the law. My mother hadn't heard from Paul in days, so we began searching and eventually found him, in jail. After numerous inquiries, we were able to piece together what had happened. On June 29, Paul was partying in a hotel room along with two other men and five women. The police received a complaint of a disturbance when the party got too loud. When they entered the room, the police found not only that one of the partygoers was wanted on a previous warrant, but also a bag containing twenty-eight grams of crack cocaine on the floor. Naturally, no one in the room claimed it. All, including Paul, were charged with trafficking and possession of crack cocaine and possession of marijuana. Paul assured my mother of his innocence and of his confidence that the judge would release him soon. He interpreted the fact that all the other participants' bonds were quite high while his was only $20,000 as evidence that the judge understands that Paul is just a dishwasher who could never afford such drugs, who had merely gone to the hotel room to borrow some money and have a few beers. It remains to be seen whether the judge is as sympathetic to his plight as Paul believes. At present, Paul remains in the Farber County Jail, awaiting his fate.

* * * * *

One day my daughter Karyn asked about death and heaven. I was caught off guard, but explained that when she dies, her soul will go to heaven where she will live and be quite happy. When asked about the dining conditions there, I attempted to explain that I wasn't sure what they ate in heaven, but that McDonald's, Burger King, and other fast food establishments don't exist there. Hours later, Karyn approached me with a very concerned look on her face. "Mommy, I don't want to die. There aren't any kitchens in heaven."

I've found myself thinking often about my daughter's innocent remark and about Paul, who, in spite of everything, I'm grateful is alive and functioning in whatever capacity he is able. How can I explain to Karyn, who cannot imagine a world without kitchens, that a heaven without them is still a wonderful place? How can I explain to the world that Paul, as different as he is from what most people would consider "normal," is still precious to us, and that we love him as our son, our brother, our Pomato Boy.

PART TWO
A MOTHER'S STORY

Sofia Maurer's Journal
November 1978 – October 1983

11/78–12/78 – Thanksgiving to Christmas, 1978—$500.00 on drugs.

3/17/79 – Paul at Chris's.

4/20/79 – Drug clinic (per Davis). PCP? Listless, removed.

4/24/79 – Davis Hospital – Crisis Emergency. Released (no crisis). Counselor gave report of jail substation #4, Dade Mental Health Crisis Unit, was kept in jail overnight, taken to crisis center, then hostile, to Davis.

4/29/79 – Vandalized van of visiting cousin at next door neighbor's. Paid $340 for three slashed tires. Later asked to pay $489 for damages, but cannot. Police questioned, realized Paul unstable. Baker Acted to vet's hospital. Was interviewed, requested he remain. After running out of the building, he returned and was admitted overnight but fled the next day.

5/2/79 – Doctor at Highland Park Hospital interviewed Paul and suggested outpatient at vet's hospital since his is private and expensive. Paul refused to go to the VA. Appointment was made with another doctor for follow up ($60 per visit) as suggested by Highland Park Doctor. Paul would not go.

5/79 – CHI (Crisis Health Intervention) – Paul spoke to counselor who made an appointment for him to see a psychiatrist, Dr. Porter. Counselor thinks Paul is on the verge of a breakdown.

5/15/79 – Dr. Porter at Crisis Help. Saw Paul for a ten-minute evaluation. Felt he was "together." Come back next week. Paul now involved in writing up research and invention for machine to read the mind. Feels such machine is controlling him. Stays up nights writing invention and list of people to report to FBI.

5/23/79 – Goes to bank, writes check (no funds in account) for neighbor to go to Washington, D.C. to obtain patent. Neighbor has no ticket in his name, is refused flight, cashed $20 check in Paul's name, comes back by taxi ($17).

5/24/79 – Dr. Porter is shocked with Paul, who is in great distress. Prescribes medication three times a day. Oldest brother, Phillip, takes Paul to Dade to speak with science teacher to explain that such a machine is not credible. As Dr. Porter said, Paul does not believe. Sleeps soundly for the first time in days. Is up at 5:00 a.m. and gone by 7:00.

5/79 – Paul started a job but did not finish. Will get someone else. Placed classified ad with Miami Herald for ten days, $150. Called by Herald worker and cancelled in time.

"Looking for L. Pardo. I've got some info about machine once used to tap the mind that will benefit. Used to work at Thurman's till two wks ago. Help you and me."

5/79 – Drives Buick with bad water pump resulting in $400 repair. Owes $100 to Cal Stewart. Did not go to second court appearance at court. Possible dismissed.

6/7/79 – Per Judge Milton's secretary, bench warrant for Paul's not appearing in court May 22 (driving without a license) has been pulled. When new date has been set, contact judge and arrange for a letter indicating Paul's instability from doctor in order to cancel appearance and ticket. Case #605526T

6/21/79 – New trial date set for June 28 with Judge Stevens. Spoke to secretary who said to obtain letter from Crisis Health regarding Paul and to submit it in person to the judge at the trial. Paul need not attend. Can be mailed but must reach her before the 27th when files leave justice building for Cutler Ridge. Presently taking medicine: Trilafon—8 mg four times a day and Cogentin—2 mg once a day.

6/22/79 – Counselor saw Paul for the first time. Continue with prescriptions. Will see him next Thursday at 12:30 and will give letter for court the same day. Present medicine will take a few months to stabilize Paul after which he will be easier to work with and will hopefully talk out his problems. $7 charge on sliding scale. If Paul not working, will not have a charge.

6/28/79 – Counselor was ill and did not see Paul at appointment time. However, left a letter signed by Doctor Pearl. Court appearance resulted in postponement for later date as Paul said "not guilty" since he was given ticket when not even in truck. Judge was a very fair man. Called Judge Stevens's secretary and promised to send a letter to that effect. Will continue to take his medicines.

7/19/79 – Saw counselor after four weeks. Medication of Trilafon reduced to three tablets a day, plus one Cogentin as Paul is overtired. This is a natural result as medication has lessened anxiety as he is getting his system back to normal. Will see again in three weeks. Working few hours per day.

7/79 – Stopped taking medicine the last week in July, saying it slowed him down. Was not interested in returning to Crisis for help. Slow and relaxed with little drive. Improved until he seemed back to normal and anxious to work.

9/79 -Worked for the union one week, then American Eagle one week, the last of September. Paid $100 to Kwick Check grocery store for two bad checks; $20 to Hank Lewis (+vodka gift); gave Claudia $5 for birthday and four bottles of champagne for her birthday in early October. Decided to go back into business for himself, taking on a number of small jobs, then a larger wall working from 8:00 a.m. to 8:00 p.m. for about four to five days.

10/79 – Following a week of happiness and productivity and looking wonderful on Claudia's sixteenth birthday (October 4) he regressed so rapidly that he could not work, would not leave the house, accused us of being Communists with religion as a cover, doing strange things... covering the Mexico painting of the beggar with a wet sheet, ordering a carton of cigarettes at 1:00 a.m., paying $20 for delivery, and staying up all night writing the same sentences over and over.

10/18/79 – When I arrived home at 6:00 p.m., the house was in chaos... Paul had taken a bat and knocked foot wide holes in the ceiling in about ten places and had locked himself in his room. His father came to try and talk to him and we called in Metro police who, after hearing his accusations that they were Commies, that he was King, and so on, enforced the Baker Act and took him to Davis Hospital, Crisis Center, where we waited for four hours. He was evaluated and suffering from delusions and being psychotic they planned to admit him but had no beds. At 1:30 a.m. he went by ambulance to vet's hospital where Admitting remembered him. He was seen by Dr. Callo whom he threatened calmly and told that he considered himself a genius.

10/19/79 – First week was kept in solitary room, did not cooperate or mix with others. Believed dead body was still in ceiling area. Would not touch or be touched by family; would not use a pen. Second week said "federal powers" had been lifted, could now write and was able to touch and kiss hello when visited. Doctors, social worker, nurses all feel he needs a few weeks to remain with them. Paul slowly starts to cooperate, but does not want to remain.

11/1/79 – Court hearing – In spite of testimony from hospital staff, as well as written evidence of Paul's instability and hostility, defense attorney, in defending Paul's civil rights, appeals to judge, saying that with medication Paul could be an outpatient. Judge says he is to remain only one week at which time he will move in with his father.

11/4/79 – When I visited Paul he was very sleepy which he says is due to the medication. He has been calling many times to get numbers of future prospects for work and is sounding full of stress again.

11/5/79 – Spoke to social worker who feels Paul is not cooperating and wishes he would "sign" himself back in. Have agreed to meeting at hospital.

11/7/79 – Meeting at hospital with Paul's father and father's new wife, doctor, and Paul. Paul will be discharged tomorrow and become "outpatient" of Crisis Center in Hialeah as he will be living with father and stepmother. Paul was happy and smiling and anxious to leave. Has been advised that he can commit himself in at any time he feels he might need help and can also sign himself out on his own. Must take medication for six months on order of the court. Is hoping to get right back to work with help from his father in getting his license, insurance, truck.

11/79–12/79 – Paul stays with his dad on and off for a week. Gets help in financing a new truck, insurance, and his father helps him get back in business. However, he cannot accept the rules of home by 6:00 p.m., no going out in the evenings, and so on. Stays in a motel a few days, returns home, and promises once again not to do drugs. He stops taking medicine and slowly regresses, climaxing by Christmas when he does not get $500 from a job, which he planned to use for presents. At his uncle's on Christmas Eve, he is sad and opens no presents awaiting him, nor does he join in our celebration dinner and presents. A few days later, Claudia and I talk him into opening gifts and he is pleased like a child.

1/80 – Paul is now reading the Bible and believes he can project into another's mind, and can read people's mind with his special gifts. Is up much of the night... covers up the Mexican Beggar Woman painting with a wet sheet and puts it into his room... wakes me in the middle of the night to tell me to leave the premises, etc. culminating in his anger over the phone with an employer... breaks kitchen window, throws a chair across room. Dan is worried for everyone's safety, especially Claudia (16) and baby Jillian (4) who is Dan's daughter. We call in police who say they have no grounds to take him in and suggest ex parte order from court.

During these weeks he goes with his father to vet's hospital where he refuses to commit himself and they won't take him without cooperation as this will not help him and only cause paperwork. One evening he goes there with me and we speak to Dr. Degas in vet hospital Crisis. He is aggravated that Paul won't help, even to give his social security number. But the doctor spoke to me for nearly an hour and is most kind and helpful, saying the cause, drugs or otherwise, is not important at this time but that he needs help. Suggest he takes two Thorazine (Chlorpromazine – 100 mg) at night or Trilafon three times a day (16 mg, for total of 48 mg per day).

1/4/80 – His father goes to court and obtains a court order to have Paul taken to hospital, for his sake and ours. Detectives take him to veterans hospital where, during admission, he becomes angry and the doctor calls to say he has run out of the hospital and is gone. He walks all the way home, waking me at 4:00 a.m. He is tired and goes to sleep. We call police who advise us, incorrectly, that the ex parte is over once they deliver him to the hospital. The police again pick him up and take him to veterans hospital.

During the next few weeks he is under the care of Dr. Ford and nurse Laura. At first he cooperates and is pleased that they will start lithium treatments, which other doctors have felt was not meant for him (meant for deep depression). However, he does not complete full series to establish his level and is taken off treatment. Drugs are found in his urine (obtained from patients who bring it in off the streets when returning from the weekend). As a result, he is placed on restriction and we cannot visit him for over a week. Phillip and I bring him cigs, food, and some clothes when he is allowed to give up hospital clothes. He becomes increasingly low, walks like a robot, and sometimes has a twitch around his mouth. He looks sad and is distant from everyone.

1/4/80 – He now starts Prolixin shots instead of pills. The shot (50 mg or 2 cc) is to be given every three weeks. Sometimes given Thorazine (50 mg) at bedtime. This is for treatment of paranoia and psychotic condition.

1/24/80 – Consultation at hospital with Paul in attendance. Dr. Ford, Hal Jimson, nurse Laura. They say he does not cooperate and he is very quiet and sad.

1/30/80 – Now wearing regular clothes and being allowed to go to dinner. He slips out and takes a cab home. I pay the $14 and he is now home AMA (against medical advice) and without hospital approval.

2/14/80 – Paul goes to CHI Clinic and is given Prolixin shot from Dave. This clinic is held every Wednesday and Paul goes again March 5 and is responding well. Dave cuts down on strength of shot and has Paul return every two weeks instead of three.

3/80–4/80 – He is doing better all the time and is working and coming out of his low feelings. He continues to go for shots.

6/80 – Paul is not working. Is on drugs—pot, cocaine. Feels guilty and low at times. Calls everyone to borrow money. Bad contacts... Garry, Cal, Belinda.

7/22/80 – Turns self in for theft of rifle, stereo, bow and arrow set, radio. Anticipated release. Instead, was booked on grand larceny and theft. Detective was very kind and advised us to go to the bond hearing the next day at the Metro Justice Building. Paul was released into "pre-trial custody of court."

8/6/80 – Arraignment date – Case dismissed as charges were dropped. These were acquaintances of Belinda and were of questionable background. They were compensated by insurance. Paul returned bow set and radio to detectives. Cal sold the rifle and stereo but denied being part of the deal to police.

8/1–8/8/80 – Paul receives Prolixin shot at CHI. On the 19th Paul tried to admit himself for addictive drugs. This occurred on two separate occasions. Also complained of severe headaches and on two other occasions we went to the VA hospital for treatment. They suggested he return in the day to seek help. Most kind.

8/23/80 – Realized my silver candelabra, silver tray and tea set were missing as well as Dan's gold coffee service tray and gold butter dish. Called police. Later found Paul had stolen and sold Dan's things for cocaine; silver of mine found in Paul's room. Called police back; detective recognized and realized Paul had "helped" in the past, therefore no charges and the detective would "follow up" on gold. The detective never answered calls from me nor Dan, even though Paul had told him at whose house he had taken the gold. Told Paul to leave house (he called me Communist), locked house; and Claudia, Dan, and I left. That evening, Paul called police, threatened suicide, and was taken by ambulance and admitted to VA hospital.

8/23–9/12/80 – VA hospital – Dr.Azor, Dr. Tanner, nurse Laura and social worker all work with Paul. On September 3 he runs out of the hospital and walks home five hours. Told him he had to return and could not remain at home. After dinner, Claudia and I take him back where he is greeted and seems able to fit in easily and not unhappily. However, he has not made Group 2, which he would have done had he not left (#3 is highest) and he loses all privileges. On September 11 we have a conference at the hospital with Paul, Drs. Azor and Tanner, Laura, social worker, and me. They advise Paul that he cannot live at home until he proves himself... stays off drugs, gets a job, straightens out. Dr. Azor tells him that if he does not do so, he will end up a vegetable or in a hospital.

9/12/80 – He goes to the welfare office but will not accept the boarding home they offer as it is in the north end of town. Instead he comes home and is not allowed in. He sleeps in the yard and looks for a job. He is more than a little surprised to find that he is on his own and people do not trust him nor want to give him money. He can't find a job.

9/20/80 – After one week of sleeping outside and working half a day cleaning at Kimball Inn and one day at carwash, he is low at finding no regular work. I allow him back in with the understanding he is to work, stay off drugs, and help at home.

9/23/80 – Applies in Perrine for welfare. His folder was sent there from another office indicating they will allow for six to eight weeks of help until he is employed again. On the 12th they had given him $31 as one week's allotment. The welfare department will send someone out this week to check our house for rooming conditions for Paul.

10/1/80 – Paul and I visit Social Security office in Perrine to fill in papers with the possibility of receiving future Social Security benefits. We also visit the welfare office but Mrs. Niles is busy. We go to CHI Clinic for Paul's shot of Prolixin... by then Mrs. Niles speaks with us on the phone at 4:30 saying she is unable to meet with us. I visit Winnipeg for two weeks during which time Paul is to attend the CHI Clinic on a daily basis from 9:00 a.m. to 2:00 p.m., with a bus to pick him up and deliver him home each day. The bus arrives each morning while I am away but Paul does not go to the clinic.

11/80 – Social Security sets up two appointments with Paul to be examined by their psychiatrist, Dr. Ivans, but he does not keep either date. We make another time at which I agree to drive him there to be sure he attends.

11/11/80 – Paul keeps his 9:00 a.m. appointment with Dr. Ivans, psychiatrist who evaluates him for the Social Security office and later tells me that he doubts that Paul will receive disability, but will try to obtain medical coverage for him to receive help as he is definitely schizophrenic with long-standing personality disorders and needs help badly. He himself would see him at $35 per half (individual) hour, adding that he also needs group therapy (or drug rehabilitation—at VA).

11/14/80 – Paul and I visited Mrs. Niles at the welfare office. She is very kind and draws Paul out. He gets teary and says he will not take drugs, but cannot stop pot. She says she can only help if he will attend CHI clinic or similar as he must try to be a useful person on his own. She sends us a $52 check for one month as help, adding that if he does not cooperate, that is it. She makes an appointment for an interview for food stamps.

CHI – Dave meets us early for the Prolixin shot as Paul did not get it as scheduled. He speaks with Mrs. Niles then calls us in and talks with us. He lays it on the line to Paul telling him that what he believes to be ESP is actually "psychotic" and that people are put into hospitals for just that reason and adds that if Paul does not stop with drugs and does not get help, he will end up in the hospital or jail. Paul says he would see Dave only, not attend the clinic, to which Dave will not agree.

11/17/80 – Mrs. Chester of Social Security office suggests that I contact Fellowship House where I speak to Jean who assigns us to orientation on Wednesday, 11/26 at 10:30 a.m. He tells me they deal with mental illness on a vocational, social, and rehabilitative basis, with support from one another.

11/26/80 – Fellowship House orientation – Counselor takes the necessary information to see about Paul joining. He needs release from vet hospital and CHI. December 4 he returns for an interview with the counselor, and is scheduled to see her again on December 18. The program is good in that there is no pressure to work and much encouragement is given. He seems interested in the social aspect... playing pool, etc.

Paul's days are long and he goes to bed "so the next day will come faster." He goes every two weeks for Prolixin shot and seems to be improving. Is anxious to afford gifts at Christmas for family but cannot face work... tries to work on cars in Homestead with Wendall and Bruce, but lasts only a couple of hours.

12/9/80 - Per appointment through Mrs. Niles (welfare), we go to Perrine Food Stamp where we speak with Mrs. Urbanik, who gives Paul full month of December food stamps totaling $62. He is to go back in January to arrange for next stamp allotment.

12/15/80 – Social Security letter arrives, denying benefits. Paul plans to re-apply even though it is likely that he will be eligible.

12/18/80 – Fellowship House – Paul sees Dr. Mansur, psychiatrist, as part of his application. He says the doctor tells him an operation will remove the voices in his mind. When I speak with the counselor she tells me this is not so... Paul suggests such an operation. No decision has been made as yet about acceptance of Paul and they have doubts as to whether he will benefit from their program as he only wants the social end, saying he cannot sit still for the morning session to train him for work. Says he wants to go to the beaches, and smoke pot in the evenings.

12/26/80 – CHI – When receiving his Prolixin shot he complains of severe headaches, and Dave suggests a neurological workup, not given there, which would be over $200. I call Dr. Azor at VA and he tells me that he will arrange for Paul to have tests there in an inpatient ten- to twelve-day period.

Sacred Heart Hospital – One evening, Paul walks there because his headache is so bad. They give medication, plus prescription for sore throat. He went there in spite of no hospital insurance, and later receives a bill for $90.

12/29/80 – VA hospital – We go to emergency and are lucky to run into Dr. Ray who had seen Paul previously. He gives a prescription to counteract the itching, which he says is a side effect of Prolixin, and should be substituted for Cogentin. Also gives a prescription (both obtained for free at VA) for headaches to last until Paul is admitted Monday for neuro tests. Tells Paul his life is passing by and he should cut down on cigs, drinking, drugs, or it will do much harm. Claudia and I both think he is "together" much of the time, but every so often he makes a complete turn. Wakes one evening to ask me to take him to Judge Hanson to get a warrant for the government to stop putting voices in his head. Tells me he can hear them, and one night they send someone with a machete to get him. I tell him to leave his door open and leave a light on in the hall all night.

1/5–1/6/81 – Admitted to VA to undergo neurological workup through Dr. Azor in psycho ward. The doctor and nurses who remember Paul are pleased that he is doing so well in appearance. Three days later no testing has been done and he is not happy in surroundings and signs himself out of hospital. Dr. Azor says not to worry, that if things are worse we can admit him again. However, he is inclined to think the headaches are more from stress than neurological.

1/81 – Paul seems to be coming along well and seldom has complaints of voices and headaches. He even tries to get work but then becomes worried and backs down. We have received three checks from welfare for $52 and Mrs. Niles is trying to get him into Fellowship where there will be structured help.

1/26/81 – Paul has a fight with Phillip because Phillip will not give him money for pot. Phillip calls police who give a warning to Paul. I tell him he must leave the house and he is not cooperating. He sleeps out in the cold Monday night, in a van Tuesday night, and Wednesday after midnight begs to return with the promise he will attend CHI clinic.

1/30/81 – Attends orientation at CHI but after speaking with Mrs. Bailey who is in charge he explains his attendance is by way of "punishment" and he will only attend a week. After speaking with her we agree that he would not benefit with this attitude and she suggests he may need drug counseling rather than what CHI offers.

The Center (previously Genesis House) is suggested by Teresa Wick. Spoke with Mindy Fay who says Paul will have to call her and set up an appointment himself. Counseling is on a one-to-one basis and he can be seen once or twice a week, with a minimum of $6 per visit which must be paid, even from his welfare check.

2/81 – Welfare – Mrs. Niles stops monthly checks as he is not attending CHI nor trying to help.

2/81 – Dr. Getty – Paul walks into her office complaining of headaches. She gives a prescription (not to be renewed) and sends him to a neurologist and sets up appointment at Sacred Heart for EKG test. He does not pay her and after discussing situation with her she suggests we continue with CHI and usual pursuit of VA and Social Security.

2/18/81 – Dr. Hoekstra reads tests taken at Sacred Heart for $50 and sees us for an appointment for $115. He says Paul needs psychiatric help and is all right neurologically. Will send report to VA and wherever we wish. I paid the $50 charge.

2/18/81 – JAIL – Paul and Garry siphon gas from a neighbor's car. Man shoots gun, calls police, boys go to jail. Paul is free in my custody on 2/19 after staying overnight. Garry put in jail as the car is stolen.

2/20/81 – Paul and Cal take cigarettes and stereo out of stolen car. Reported by neighbor... taken to jail... overnight and judge will not release Paul. $150 paid to bondsman. Bad experience after which Paul regresses and stress along with the many voices in his head increase.

2/26/81 – SECOND DEGREE BURNS – on left palm and fingers from hot bacon grease while cooking. In extreme pain, so much so he will not leave for hospital as he needs ice every minute. Says it is better the next few days but is very sensitive and swollen.

2/27/81 – Beaten with rubber mallet by a boy who says Paul stole his pot plants months ago. His burnt hand was bleeding and right hand swollen, with a knot on his head. We went to emergency at VA hospital from 3:00 a.m. until 8:30 Saturday morning. Finger broken on left hand. Surgeon peeled dead skin, wrapped it and gave us material to change daily, plus six prescriptions (vitamins, penicillin, silvadene cream, etc).

3/2/81 – We tried to see an orthopedic doctor at the VA per instructions on Monday morning but the wait was three to four hours so we could not stay. Very helpful lady in charge of Admitting-Outpatient, says to continue trying for aid from VA benefits.

3/5–3/17/81 – All court appearances regarding siphoning of gas, theft of stereo from stolen car. On Friday 3/6 appearance, Paul goes to judge's chambers and tell of voices, FBI taping mind, etc. before judge, secretary, attorney, and court reporter. As a result he is assigned Bill King by the State and is sent for a psychiatric evaluation to Dr. Eugene at the Professional Arts Center at 8:00 a.m. on 3/13. He reports to the judge and Paul is to get into a program for help, such as Fellowship. Trial on both counts will be April 20.

5/16/81 – Judge dismissed the case of siphoning gas as no witness nor police attended.

5/18/81 – Dr. Armand Romano, Ph.D., will see Paul on a weekly basis, $20 instead of $50. Will compile information and decide what course to follow.
5/16/81 - $20.00
5/27/81 - $20.00
6/1/81 - $20.00
6/1/81 – Court with Judge Dea. Dismissed by reason of insanity. Court date for 6/29/81 with reports from Dr. Eugene and Dr. Romano regarding the progress of Paul.
6/3/81 – Receive Prolixin shot at 6:00 pm at CHI Clinic. Then visit a friend. At 9 p.m. in front of Claudia, cannot make sounds, nor walk straight, then collapses into a coma. Paramedics take him to Sacred Heart Hospital emergency room where he remains in coma, with overdose of Quaaludes. Is admitted on the 4th, still in coma. Remains in coma for nineteen hours. When he awakens in Critical Care Unit where we must stay with him constantly, he admits he had planned the entire thing... went to work and obtained advance of money... bought $100 for fifty Quaaludes... Gave four to Cal, then took forty-six when I went to practice for Marie's wedding... was sorry he had not died as he wanted to see God and could not stand the voices talking to him all the time. He cried and said he would try again. Dr. Maguire, a psychiatrist, came to evaluate him in the hospital and said he was psychotic and suicidal, and needed help.

Dear Dr. Dennis:

On behalf of my son Paul I wish to thank you for your help during his emergency stay at Sacred Heart Hospital. I have only the very highest praise for the attention given to my son last week. His mind is in very fragile condition and no matter what the future holds for him I shall never forget the kindness from you, Mrs. Michaels, and the many nurses and doctors who attended him.
God bless you.

Sincerely,

Sofia Maurer

6/5/81 – Sacred Heart Hospital agrees to write off his bill (over $1,000) to charity. As he cannot remain there since they are not a psychiatric facility, he is taken by ambulance to CHI Clinic in Perrine (rather than VA, which would have been the better choice) with the hopes of being admitted to Coral Reef Hospital. At Sacred Heart he was given intravenous feedings and cared for. At CHI a doctor saw him a few minutes on Friday, then a weekend substitute (Dr. Dennis) saw him once on Saturday and once on Sunday. He rebelled and left the facility three times in twenty-four hours. Greatly agitated he called doctors, hospitals, lawyers, to try to get shock treatments. Finally he returned on Sunday, called Judge Dea, and remained at home.

6/8/81 – Judge Dea told Paul to come to court on Monday at 9:00 a.m. We were joined by Dr. Romano. The Judge suggested Paul be committed for one month, but Armand Romano suggested a week at Davis to which the judge agreed. After waiting three hours at Davis Crisis, he was evaluated by Dr. White as not needing immediate care, and was sent home. EVERYONE was amazed at this, the doctors, judge, and lawyer.

6/81 – CHI – Paul starts weekly CHI Prolixin shots (1.2 cc) instead of every other week, and is seen by Dr. Porter. He slowly calms down, still hears voices, tries to get marijuana whenever possible. One evening we go to the emergency room at CHI as he complains of severe headaches. His blood pressure is high (bottom reading ninety) and is given medicine to lower pressure and pills for headache. When Dr. Porter sees him a few days later, says to stop these pills and try to get to normal status with Prolixin. Says Paul is still after drugs. Pressure is down.

6/81 – Continues weekly shots and is calmer, relaxed. Still hallucinates, but less often. Tries to work doing a stone job but lasts only a few days. Stress and tenseness increase and he quits. He will not listen to suggestions to take small jobs for a few hours per day to see if he could cope.

7/29/81 – Paul is scheduled for a Social Security hearing to obtain benefits. Through referral from the bar association we meet David Zimmerman, attorney, who will represent Paul at hearing. Dr. Romano, who sees Paul every week or so, will also attend.

8/6/81 – Final hearing in court with Judge Dea, who takes case off calendar. Letter to be sent to the judge from Doctor Romano telling of Paul's progress.

9/1/81 – Social Security hearing with Judge Elizondo. Zimmerman represents Paul and Dr. Romano speaks in his behalf saying Paul's problems are long standing, at least to elementary school days, that ***he is not a drug addict by his very nature, but that he turns to this as a means of medication and an outlet of relief.*** He also states that Paul needs at least one year in a controlled program in order to cope and that he is no longer able to help, but that it would be impossible for Paul to work in his state of mind and that the most he could handle would be a few weeks after which he would become tense, miss work, and finally quit or be fired under his present tension. Judge Elizondo said we would hear within four to six weeks as to her verdict.

10/1/81 – Dr. Oscar Davidson, Highland Park Hospital, suggests a CAT scan and blood test to rule out brain damage in the first and "Wilkinson Disease" in the second. If these are negative, then will try shock treatments. Feels Paul's problems are basically drug induced from nearly three years ago, with his behavioral problems as secondary.

10/5/81 – Cedars of Lebanon Hospital – Mother and Jeff take Paul for the CAT scan ($415 paid by Mother), which turns out to be negative. The blood test is not to be determined for up to two weeks. Paul is to go to Highland Park on October 11 for observation and shock treatments. He becomes distressed and at times during the week says he will not go. $2,940 for ten days for doctor and hospital... shocks extra.

10/11/81 – Highland Park – Paul is admitted Sunday and starts daily shock treatments on Monday. Throughout the week he leaves once and wants to sign himself out, which they do not agree with.

10/12/81 – Social Security Office in Perrine – Mrs. Occopinti takes the current info on Paul and I sign the paper for his checks to be made out to me, per Judge Elizondo, as he is not capable of handling money. Her estimate is about $170 per month with the first check retroactive for about a year. He will be eligible for Medicaid, which will cover prior unpaid bills.

10/12–10/22/81 – Highland Park Hospital for ten days at approximately $4,000 paid by Mother. Receives eight shock treatments, ECT, in hopes of getting rid of the voices he hears. He runs away once and is placed in ICU to prevent this again. As he is somewhat sedated from the treatments and daily Prolixin, he does not partake in group therapy or dance sessions, etc. However, when I visit daily he is smiling and calm and joins in on Family Nights (two Tuesday evenings) and even dances with Mother and once with me. We cannot afford to keep him there although both Dr. Davidson and Dr. Cameron say he needs at least another eight treatments and a controlled environment for a longer time. When he receives Medicaid we hope to readmit him. He returns home and becomes worried at not being able to find work. His memory has lapses due to ECT treatments ... does not remember Dr. Romano, judge and Social Security hearing, and so on.

10/27/81 – Does not call nor come home. After checking police and crisis centers there is no information.

10/28/81 – Call from Dr. Reagan, cardiologist at Dade Hospital. Paul was found unconscious outside Rizzo's Bar. He could not be revived and police brought him into emergency where he remained in a coma, then awoke and was psychotic. Although toxicology reports stated liquor and no drugs, I spoke with Michael Rizzo who said he saw Paul take a bootleg Quaalude and found another on the ground where Paul had been. Paul did not remember these, only drinking. I spent the night in a private room, after his being in ICU, as he could not be alone. The next morning Mother and Jeff stayed with him.

> Dear Mr. Jay,
>
> I am writing on behalf of my son, Paul Maurer, who was brought in your hospital last week. He was brought to the emergency room in a coma, then to the ICU unit, then to the fifth floor. The treatment and kindness from your staff was superlative. This was particularly true of both Dr. Reagan and Ms. Evelyn Buckingham who had such understanding and compassion. Through their special efforts Paul was transferred to the psychiatric ward at Veterans Hospital where he remains under their care. For nearly three years Paul has been a sick young man and although we hear of help for mental problems, it is not always available, and seldom so graciously

Claudia M. Jones Ph.D.

> *handled. Regardless of Paul's progress we shall always be grateful for the help of Dade Hospital.*
>
> *Sincerely,*
>
> *Sofia Maurer*

10/29/81 – Veterans hospital – Through the good work of Evelyn Buckingham, social worker at Dade Hospital, along with Dr. Reagan and Dr. Azor, we were able to arrange with the office of Dr. Knapp, Chief of Outpatient at VA, to admit Paul as he is feared to be not only psychotic but "self-destructive, unable to cope with stress." His attitude is the best they have seen for the first time he attends group sessions, plays cards, and is sociable. He has been told he will be there at least twenty-one days.

11/3/81 – Paul has mumps. Dr. Sidney speaks on the phone asking me to take him home as they cannot keep him on the floor while he is contagious. As I refuse to do so, fearing they would not take him back to VA, they put Paul in a separate room. There is a chance it may not be mumps but merely swelling which he had a number of times as a teen, lasting a few days then disappearing.

11/3–11/7/81 – Paul remains in isolation room with possibility of mumps. He is in great spirits and doing well; however, when put back in the ward with roommates who upset him, screaming and defecating etc., he becomes upset and talks of returning home. Slowly he settles down, is kept on Prolixin. He stops attending group therapy, does not progress to next Group II so on his birthday, November 11, we celebrate on the floor rather than at the Veteran's Day Celebration in the lobby.

11/13/81 – Runs out of the VA hospital, takes a cab home, gives my gold watch as payment of $34 to be held until we pay. We convince him to return to be discharged the following week with medical approval and medicine. He agrees, returns to the hospital without punishment as Dr. Azor has promised.

11/18/81 – Dismissed from VA with Prolixin pills for two weeks, then to return to CHI for injections. Orally 10 mg (two pills) in the morning and 20 mg (four pills) at night. Injections were 37.5 mg (1½ cc) weekly.

11/81–12/81 – Paul receives two months of Medicaid, which is then cancelled until Medicare takes effect in March or September.

His first check from SSI for $360 he takes and forges my signature, giving me $120 for the month and spends the rest.

12/15/81 – Dr. Philie at Dade Hospital is in charge of an alcohol and drug program to rehabilitate. She interviews Paul but says that their six-week program for $5,000 does not permit drugs, including his weekly Prolixin shot, and feels that this program would not be for Paul as his is a psychiatric problem first, with the drugs a secondary aspect.

12/16/81 – Linda Barr, Highland Park, counsels for their drug program under Dr. Frank, speaks with Paul and agrees with Dr. Philie's analysis and says his drugs are to alleviate his mental state. She suggests putting him in the psychiatric ward for the rest of December while he still has Medicaid but not in the Addictive Treatment Center. However, Paul refuses to go.

12/81 – Paul is happy to be home and on December 14 we pick up his large Social Security check for over $2,000. He gives $1,000 to me for the escrow shortage since he owes me for many debts over the past three years. He has $200 with which he buys clothes, presents for the family for Christmas, and so on.

During this time he gives my family Bible to a waitress at Lum's to hold until he pays his $50 debt to her. He sells Phillip's stereo for which I paid $25 to redeem in the summer. My grass cutter he gives to Mrs. Van Dyke, for which I pay $15. All this goes to eat out, buy drinks and pot. He is not trying to better his condition, saying he is happy in his life. It is difficult to get him to cut the grass, clean his bath and room, and so on. He does so, but only with much urging.

1/10/82 – Paul asks for $25 for pot and when I refuse, he becomes angry and calls me names. He will not leave when I ask him to do so, keeping Phillip from fighting with him for what he has said, and finally I call 911 and the police come and order him to leave. He does so, and spends the day calling everyone... his dad, Mother, friends, to try and find a place to live. Ends up at the VA hospital where he is evaluated and spends the night.

1/11/82 – Mary Shelley, a social worker at the VA, speaks with Paul trying to place him in a rooming house, which he declines. He calls places all day and finally finds a little apartment for rent in Little Havana. I drive him there after work, sign for a week's rent ($50) plus $50 security (to be refunded) and $40 for gas for the stove. He is very pleased and I go shopping with him for $30 groceries and help him move in. He plans to get a job.

1/12/82 – Paul is arrested on Eighth Street trying to buy $5 worth of pot and since he has no ID he is taken to jail. When I arrive to post $25 bond, he is being released on his own. When he goes to court on February 5, the judge and the attorneys decide not to adjudicate if he pleads no contest. Therefore he has no record of guilt. Bill King appears with him as a friend, not appointed by the court. He and the arresting officer warn Paul to stay straight.

1/82 – Paul moves back to his home but he is unable to manage on his own. He works as a busboy at Cap d'Antibes for three days, at a Wendy's for less than a week, and is in my office almost every day. He puts his father's TV in a pawn shop and stops trying to find work, coming home on weekends. Having spent a few hundred dollars for rent and food, and not improving his way of life, I agree to his return although his brothers, sister, and our friends think this is not a good decision.

2/82–3/82 – Social Security disability checks arrive and Paul forges my name and takes the money. When his large Social Security check arrives for over $2,000, he gives it to a friend to whom he owes money ($500) and he vanishes from home for a few days. After speaking with the Social Security office they advise me not to file for a lost check as Paul would be prosecuted and I change the mailing address for future checks to my office. With many phone calls, Paul's friend brings back a personal check, minus $150 which he advanced to Paul, plus $100 paid toward the $500 debt, with a promise to pay monthly. However, Paul said the money was for drugs and secondly, he forged my name on the following month (April) check. On 3/10 I changed the mailing address to my office... HA! Up to sixty days to process. If 3rd of month is on a weekend or holiday, check is delivered the prior bank day.

4/82 – Paul spends entire $360 from forged check in one night. Phillip sees someone pick him up in a car... Paul dressed in his new three-piece Easter suit... he later says he spent it on champagne, so we figure the money went for drugs, a girl, and booze. It is very discouraging as he never seems to learn or profit from his experiences. His behavior becomes bizarre, staying up nights, sleeping all day, and later he admits to taking hits of acid. One night he awakens me to say he has tried to commit suicide by injecting air into his veins but says it didn't work. He asks to go to the VA hospital, but later changes his mind.

4/12/82 – VA hospital –Paul is in mental pain, says he tried to swallow Raid bug killer but just threw up. We go to the VA where he is admitted for psychiatric evaluation at midnight. Remains the following day and then on the 14th he leaves against medical advice. I spoke with the doctor, who wanted him to remain and says he needs help but cannot be forced to stay.

4/82 – Rizzo's – Paul starts a brick job on a wall at Rizzo's Liquor Store on US 3 where he is already in debt for $100 to the owner, Michael Rizzo. He is quite enthused at first and is given $50 on two consecutive nights by Michael; he spends it at the bar each night and by the third day is not fit to work there. At the same time he starts a job for Frank McCourt who was the owner of Kimball Inn, and is told he will receive a truck if and when he finishes stoning the entire house on all four sides. He lasts there a few more days, then quits. He says Frank gave him $10 plus a previous $35 for the entire front, adding that he was in debt $400 over the past few years. He is now low again and spends much time in his room. Paul charges $150 (on my MasterCard) for four calls to California to a service that dealt with sexual fantasies, etc., by obtaining my number from a paid bill. As a result, I called there and asked them not to accept the calls, and also cancelled out my MasterCard, which was over $1,100. In addition, he called California so often that I am forced to disconnect the phones during the day. He called at all hours during the nights and the four MasterCard calls averaged $35 each. The company is questionable as they did not wish to speak with me and even said it was the wrong number.

4/28/82 – Social Security computer update tells me that Paul will be eligible for Medicare in September 1982, at which time there is a $260 deductible, the hospital is paid 100% and the doctors 80%. We will still go to the CHI Clinic every other week for Prolixin shot and also Paul takes Benadryl to help prevent the itching, which is a side effect. He still hears his voices.

5/11/82 – Visiting at Chris's when Dan called to tell me to come home as Paul was dancing in his room to loud music and carrying on conversations alone in his room. When I arrived he denied taking drugs and said he was just happy. He would not come with me to the VA hospital but ran out of the house; I later stopped by

Claudia M. Jones Ph.D.

Frank McCourt's where Paul was sitting and talking to Bill who lives at Frank's. He seemed subdued but was upset to see me and told me to leave. He slept in someone's yard that night but then moved into McCourt's for which I gave him a $50 check for the week. McCourt would not allow Paul to take any drugs and drink only wine and supposedly planned to buy a truck so Paul and Bill could go into the stone business. However, Paul smoked half a joint and was told to leave after four nights there. He stole the check, forged Frank's signature, and bought a tent, which he set up across the street at Mr. Leeds's house. He said that he had done the work and was never paid fully by Frank and did not feel he owed him anything. Paul started to work a few nights at Lum's washing dishes, and then again on Saturday and Sunday morning and was to be on the payroll. I had allowed him to shower at home on a few occasions and he seemed pretty much together and was happy with the plan to work at Lum's.

5/22/82 – Paul had slept home Friday and Saturday and worked five hours on Sunday at Lum's. When he came home at 2:00 p.m. he showered and dressed to return there to see a waitress he liked. I gave him $5 and he left happily. Mother and Jeff were working around the yard and when he returned two hours later he was a different person... belligerent and wanted to go to bed. I told him he had to help carry the cuttings out front and he did so angrily for five minutes then went back to his room. Again I said he had to help or move out. He came into the garage, threatened me, called me names, and then pushed me so hard that I hurt my finger for which I went to Sacred Heart Hospital with treatment in the emergency room for a possible broken bone. It was not; I had a splint for a few days, as well as bruises. In any case, he called Jeff names and threatened him, then set up the tent across the street again. At this point I realized he could not live with us as he was a danger to all of us. Throughout the week he wandered around unshaven, sleeping one night at McCourt's where he refused to help out in the day and was told to leave. Also, he drove to his father's and borrowed $100 which he told me $50 was for a tire for Bill's car and the other $50 was "spaced out" over a few days. He called me at work to say he needed $75 to stay some place and when I said I needed more information he called me names and hung up.

5/27/82 – Paul insisted I call the police to take him to the VA hospital or he would wreck the house. They came, called an ambulance, and he was taken to the VA. He is under the care of Dr. Takemura (female) who never spoke with me nor answered my many calls.

5/27–6/3/82 – The following Thursday Paul left the VA against medical advice. He wanted to get his social security disability check from the mail and to cash and spend it, not realizing it would come to me at the office. For two nights he slept on the patio next door. We spent the weekend shopping for a room or apartment for him as neither Claudia nor Dan felt it was safe for him to stay at home. We had no luck as places were too expensive or did not want him. He came home in despair and spent an hour trying to call people for a job. Finally he reached Ed Kwiatkowski who offered him a job painting. I allowed him home again.

6/7–6/9/82 – Paul traveled over four hours a day, three buses each way to work with Ed painting a house. By the third day he was doing well and was paid $125, which made him proud. He gave me $100 to bank. There was no work for the next two days. Thursday through Sunday, restless and low.

6/12/82 – Paul attends the Lubavich's twenty-fifth wedding anniversary with Claudia and me at the Ukrainian Club and has a very good time, socializing with friends and even dancing a little. On Sunday we all attend Ukrainian church but when we arrive home he spends time in his room. He does not want to attend the Goombay Festival in the Grove with Phillip and me and asks for $20 of his money earned with Ed to go to the beach. While I am at the festival he buys syringes and insecticide and injects his arm, trying to commit suicide.

6/14/82 – 6:00 a.m., Paul awakens me in excruciating pain and tells me what he had done the previous day. We go to the VA where he remains in Admitting until 2:00 p.m. when they release him telling him to go home and just take aspirin.

6/15/82 – When I arrive home at 5:30 p.m., his arm is swollen, red, and he has a fever of 103 degrees. He is then admitted to the VA hospital where they make an incision to start draining the poison, put him in ward 9AB where he starts with an IV in his left arm until it is removed Monday the 21st. Each day a doctor or a surgeon removes the pus that has collected.

Claudia M. Jones Ph.D.

6/22/82 – The doctors say they have done their work for Paul and the psychiatrist in charge says Paul is to go to 4 AB, at which he leaves the hospital, again AMA.

7/82 – Paul insists he must have a car so I pay Peter Van Dyke $400 plus $50 for insurance plus tag and license. The car lasts two days when he sells it for $20 or $40 and some pot. A month later police come to the door tracking down the car and I explain Paul is in the VA hospital. Later the car is ditched, towed, and auctioned. Paul is home but unsettled and often low in spirits. One day my two grass cutters are gone as he owed money and gave them in exchange after a fight. His hand is injured and we spend four hours at the VA and finally are told the injury is superficial. He does not try to work at a job or at home and runs up telephone bills to California, Washington, and Virginia regarding his invention to read the mind, to Uncle William who is in the FBI in Virginia, and so on. He has a lawyer and believes he will patent his machine and make a lot of money. Phone bills are $20–$60 a month for Paul.

8/82 – Paul becomes offensive and agrees to move out as he upsets everyone at home and Claudia is now afraid of him. First he rents a room across the highway for $35 per week, but lasts only one night as everyone there is drunk and they throw bottles and what little furniture exists. Next he moves in with Guy and that lasts a week and a half.

8/16/82 – Things are closing in on Paul and he is dropped off at the house by Guy and comes knocking at the back door—I am shocked to see he has a mohawk haircut. I give him money for dinner at Lum's and he returns at 10:00 p.m. to say he has a place to stay but needs $50. I give him a check and at 3:00 a.m. he phones to say the check was stolen and he is out of gas. He manages to make it home and I give him another $50 check and he goes off with an empty gas container.

8/17/82 – VA hospital – Paul admits himself saying he felt like he was having a nervous breakdown. He is put on Haldol instead of Prolixin. He still has hallucinations but seems pleased to be there where the doctors and nurses now know him and are very kindly.

8/21/82 – Two young men come by the house to say Paul drove a girl to the hospital a week ago as she was in pain and there was no one to help, and they haven't seen the car since. Paul had driven himself to the VA in the same car and it is in the parking lot at the VA. A few days later the one boy returns with a bill for $55 for a locksmith as Paul left the key in the ignition and it was gone.

8/16/82 – Ellen Baker tells me of an alcohol and drug rehabilitation center for sixteen- to twenty-nine-year-olds called Meta Therapy. Ellen's nephew was taken to Meta Therapy where he has remained for three weeks. There are no locks and lots of love is used in rehabilitation... no communication is allowed in the beginning. The average stay is eight months, it is federally funded with a sliding scale. They check with CHI and tell me they feel sure Paul will be accepted. I am excited and have great hopes for this program.

8/23/82 – Dr. Carbone who works with Dr. Azor at the VA calls to discuss Paul with me. He feels that he is not ready for the rehabilitation center and feels Paul will be in the hospital at least for a few weeks. Paul seems to agree and is happy to see me with cigarettes, food, fruit. His medication is changed to Trilafon.

8/25/82 – Dr. Azor calls and sets up an appointment for the following day with Paul to be present. He says Paul has been delusional and ill but that the antipsychotic medicine is helping him and that for the first time Paul is cooperating and wants to be well. There is now a question of a gall bladder medicine, which he will explain in person.

8/26/82 - Conference with Dr. Azor, Dr. Largo, and nurse present with Paul and me. He is working with them for a change and will take the bladder test, which will only tell if in the future years he would benefit from what is now experimental.

9/82 – While I am on a two-week vacation in Canada, Paul leaves the hospital for a few days but is convinced to remain there and Phillip takes him back. His progress is the best in years and he remains in the VA hospital until his release on 9/30 (since 8/17). He works into a group where he enjoyed doing ceramics and returns home quite content.

10/82 – Paul does work around the house, meets some new friends at a karate school, helps sell hot dogs and stays relatively low key, while hoping to get into the Meta Therapy Rehabilitation program.

10/28/82 – Paul starts at Meta Therapy. At intake we speak with the therapist, who explains to Paul that he is in need of help. He fluctuates between remaining or returning home and I tell him that he cannot return and that I will not give him money or cigarettes as this has to be the best opportunity and chance for him. He finally agrees and we bring in his clothes, linens for bed, toilet articles, etc. He settles down and when I return later with two new prescriptions from CHI he is not in sight but attending a group session. He will not be able to call home for two weeks nor to have a visitor for four weeks. Thank God he is to be helped!

11/1/82 – Four days later Paul decides he does not want to stay there any longer. He packs his belongings, takes a cab and goes to the karate shop on Dixie Highway to his friend Don, who pays the $15 for the cab. He smokes a joint and after a few hours decides he made a mistake and wants to return. Uncle Chris takes him back and hears the discussions wherein they are about to take Paul back until he starts talking about his control of people on TV and how he can read minds, etc. As a result, the staff at Meta Therapy feels he needs psychiatric help in addition to drug rehabilitation and they dismiss him saying he can apply again in a few months if he works at stabilizing himself.

11/3/82 – Paul is upset as he found many aspects there which were to his liking, and he had made friends. We had agreed that he could not return home without some help. He spends one night sleeping in my car. Then we make an arrangement with the owner of the karate school that for $175 per month Paul can live there. We agree to try for one month.

Each morning and evening Paul comes home to bathe (there is no shower at karate) and change and to eat. He makes up a couch each night for sleeping... Don also stays there as a caretaker and has his own room. These are Paul's friends and although they are older, they seem to influence Paul so he does not do drugs and he even helps Don during the day in selling hot dogs from a stand.

11/12/82 – Social Security disability office has a hearing for Paul with Mrs. Thomas who is very kind to him and takes down info as to his stays in various hospitals over the past year. His case is reviewed. Mrs. Thomas tells us of Miami Mental Health Center and suggests we look into their facility.

11/12/82 – Mrs. Thomas advises that Medicare (Paul became eligible in September) bill January through December with $60 deductible for doctor per year, $260 deductible for hospital per year for 1982 and $304 deductible for hospital per year for 1983... then Medicare pays 80% of bill.

11/15/82 – Mark Mueller called from Tallahassee from Social Security Disability Services to say he had reviewed Paul's case from Mrs. Thomas and that he would be setting up an appointment for Paul to see a psychiatrist of whom he spoke very highly... Dr. Lopez. He was very helpful and said to call if we had any questions or problems. Paul is doing quite well, works now and then at Lum's, has applied for a job at Kwick Check, and seems content.

11/30/82 – Dr. Lopez speaks to Paul for only five or ten minutes and when I ask to speak with him he says he is in a hurry but he does say that Paul must get back on Trilafon and Benadryl which he had stopped taking. When I explained that he now has Medicare and would he continue to see him, he said that when he received and reviewed Paul's file, he would call me. The two girls working in his office were Magdalene Academy graduates and knew Claudia. The doctor was a tremendous disappointment. Dr. Maguire, who saw Paul when he had taken the Quaalude dose at Sacred Heart Hospital, did not answer my call but had his secretary say I could set up a half-hour appointment for $40 to talk to Paul but he was booked up until the first of the year with the exception of one day before Christmas, so we will not be seeing him. Spoke to Dr. Davidson who said he would admit Paul to Highland Park if he would go and to work with him and see what should be done for him. Paul was not interested.

12/2/82 – Paul says that he is going to move in with Frank and needs $200 cash by 3:30 p.m. He comes to my office to get a check plus $20 cash for food. Later I find he spent it all on drugs (cocaine and a bag of pot). Then he says he must pay $50 to Don, which he owes in order to remain at the karate place. After taking that money, I find a few days later he blew that as well. He now has gone through most of his December Social Security check and now has no place to live.

12/82 – One evening Paul calls Claudia names and refuses to leave the house unless we call the police, which we do. They say although he is talking bizarre (he says he is "special" since his name is Paul, lives on the west side of the highway, is born on Veteran's Day, etc.) they can do nothing. He agrees to leave and starts sleeping outside. He is not doing drugs and is calm and starts to be more appreciative... for a few days.

Claudia M. Jones Ph.D.

12/15/82 – Frank McCourt calls to say that Paul drove up to his house with a friend in a blue Camaro, announced to the neighbor what he was about to do in order to appear before a judge, then took a TV, stereo, watch, radio, etc.

12/16/82 – Paul was very bizarre and tense and by Thursday when we arrived at CHI for medication they said he was delusional. When we arrived home Scott Harrington and Phillip were waiting and we decided the only answer was to admit him to the VA. When the psychiatrist spoke with him he agreed that he was suffering and in great stress so he was admitted.

12/22/82 – Dr. Azor calls to say that Paul plans to leave AMA (against medical advice) and he cannot talk him out of it. He says Paul is sick and needs help but they cannot detain him if he will not agree. He then leaves the hospital. I spoke to Detective Gale and we agree that because Paul wants to be home for Christmas, she will hold off getting a warrant for his arrest as he is not cooperating with her and will not say who has the stolen goods. His other option is to return to the VA by Sunday night, or to see her at the jail Monday at 8:00 a.m.

12/23/82 - The dentist sees Paul first thing in the morning as an emergency to give him a temporary cap on an eye tooth (the original temp had fallen off and he looked bad). We were afraid he would be in the hospital or jail and so he took care of him at no charge as a Christmas gift.

12/24/82 - Christmas Eve – Paul is delusional and ranting and raving and insists on me giving him money and at Chris's he said if I didn't give him $100 he would burn the house. I left Chris's and met with the police at home. They spoke with Paul on the phone and warned him. I returned to Chris's, sang midnight Mass, and returned home. Paul returned at 5:00 a.m. but I would not let him in. He slept outside.

   ***Dr. Azor says to give Paul whatever medication (antipsychotic) that I can get a prescription for... Trilafon 8 mg three times daily instead of 16 mg two times daily... but OK as a second choice... or Thorazine 200 mg two times daily instead of three times daily. Best to have him in a controlled environment for a few months, even South Florida or Arcadia.

12/25/82 - When we return from 10:00 a.m. Mass we open presents. Later Paul appears with a dozen roses, which he bought from money earned doing yard work for Bobby who is with him and agrees to the story. During the day, a young man stops by looking for Paul who had taken off with his $300 bike. Paul shows up and says he left it in front of Lum's and of course it is no longer there so Paul now owes $300. The boy's name is Steve Haldane and he seems very presentable.

12/27/82 – Paul does not want to return to the hospital and we go to CHI and start Prolixin shots again but a smaller (0.7cc weekly dose which Dr. Porter feels is the best treatment for Paul, along with Vistaril (25mg two times daily).

12/28/82 – Through many conversations with Frank McCourt and Detective Gale, Paul confides that it is the karate group who have the goods and no charges are filed. Most of the items are then returned to the jail... to the detective. Many mixed feelings during these few weeks... burglary and theft for any reason was wrong... Paul insists Frank owed money to him for stone work... many feel that he should go to court and have a judge commit him for a period of time to control him... I feel he is headed for a bad climax and wish we could prevent it... no one wants him at home and although many are helping, we are also worried.

1/3/83 – Social Security check arrives and $200 goes to Steve Haldane for stolen bike. Paul takes remaining $170, which he says is for apartment. Within two days he is totally broke. He alternates from sleeping in the yard, to the garage, then the house. When we go for Prolixin he is given the larger dosage as the past visit is not noted on the charts. Paul occasionally helps out at Lum's in exchange for breakfast. He does odd jobs for a few dollars but spends it immediately with no thought for food or cigarettes at a future time.

1/8/83 – Paul demands that I give him a $400 check (part he says Dan owes and part as an advance). When I refuse, he threatens to break in car windows with a bat. We call the police who say they can do nothing as he has done no harm as of yet. Later, he threatens me and says he will hit me if I do not give a check. He will not let either Claudia or me into the house. He counts to five and hits me in the face... Claudia runs to a neighbor's house and calls the police. Paul counts to five again and hits me... he is screaming and has his fists ready to hit again so I agree to give him a check and go into the house and stall until the police arrive. They Baker Act him into CHI. This is Saturday. He runs out on Sunday, sleeps in our yard. Monday evening he is picked up by police and taken back. He is put into restraints and remains until he is released Tuesday evening.

1/11/83 – CHI – After returning home from being Baker Acted at CHI he says he can live at Bobby's but must pay. I take him to the bus on US 3 and a few hours later he returns saying Bobby wouldn't let him stay there while he was talking about people in his head, even though he supposedly gave Bobby cash for $45. He then sleeps in the yard with blankets when it is very cold.

1/13/83 – He says he can room at Guy's and I again give him money, $25, which he says he loans to Garry, who disappears. He is again without money or a place to live. I let him sleep in my car as it is cold and then the next few nights I let him sleep in the garage. During this period when I give him $45 and then $25, he also earns money from Rick and it is all spent... undoubtedly on pot and beer. Phillip and I agree that he should have as little help as possible in hope of getting him into the VA where they will stabilize him and then get him into a program. I cannot let him sleep in the cold, however, nor can I let him go hungry.

1/17/83 – Paul says he can move into Steve Haldane's home for a week. Steve tells me his mother has agreed. Paul is happy and packs a few things then tries to reach the Carters to be paid for work done that day in sealing stone. He expects $200 but Rick tells me later that he worked only a few hours and the work was careless and worth no more than $25. He had already given Paul $8, which was spent. When I return home from the opera, Paul is waiting, very sad. He said Steve lied, he could not stay at Steve's and he now had no money.

1/18/83 – When I return home from work Paul is waiting and has spent the $20 from Carter's on pot and beer. He is unstable. When I will not help him, he agrees to go to the VA and Phillip takes him there. A doctor with whom I speak on the phone in the VA Crisis says they will admit him that his psychological problems are such that he will be better at times, that he may also become worse. At least he will get help and I am relieved temporarily.

1/20/83 – Paul appears in my office in rain having left the VA. I refuse to give him even coffee money and advise him to return before midnight. He does not and we are again in the routine... he whiles away the days and sleeps in the garage at night. One day he is angry because he finds out that the VA may have had a hearing in Washington, D.C., (Oct. '81) without him (per a lawyer he went to see and who sent for his records) and that their decision not to give him disability is final. When he returns home Claudia will not let him in the house (he is not allowed in when I am not there at this point) and so he calls her names and kicks in the door, knocking out a panel. She is frightened and I tell her on the phone to let him in at which time he calms down. His disappointment and frustration are heavy upon him.

2/3/83 – Paul is now excited about getting back into business and buying a truck from Garry. He will not be discouraged and has me type out an agreement to pay $100 down and weekly payments of $50 to Garry. From his $371 Social Security check he pays Garry $100, another $100 goes for tools for his job with the stone yard and construction companies, and to pick up his driver's license which he left at a restaurant when he couldn't pay a $2.50 bill. When I arrive home from work he takes the last $100 to pay for a battery and voltage regulator, which the truck needed. That night he is stopped by the police and they find the license tag is stolen and that Paul does not have his license. He is taken directly to jail where he spends the night. The next day he shows up at my office, all disheveled and low in spirit, and asks for the remaining $50 to get the car out of the towing service. They do not release the truck to him as he has no title, registration, or proof of ownership. He spends the money, however, and is broke. He is discouraged at what was to have been a new start and at how badly it turned out and he will now have to go to court.

2/4/83 – When it becomes cold out and Dan will not give him any blanket to sleep outside, he calls the police to take him to CHI as he cannot cope. They sedate him and he remains there from Friday night until Sunday afternoon when he is taken by ambulance to the VA. I spoke with the same doctor who saw him in the Crisis VA on 1/18. He agrees to admit him although they are crowded.

2/7/83 – Dr. Azor says he regrets but must dismiss Paul as they are short of beds and others need help more than Paul. They give him Prolixin but he does not pick up an additional prescription.

2/9/83 – Detective Gale calls to say she wants to tell me in advance that there will be a warrant out for Paul for not returning the rest of Frank McCourt's two speakers, a TV and his father's old watch as Paul has not tried to get these back as promised. She doesn't want me to tell him that she will be there to

Claudia M. Jones Ph.D.

arrest him two days later. She is very kind and tries to make it as easy as possible for me.

2/11/83 – Detective Gale arrives at 8:30 a.m. with another detective. They handcuff Paul and he is amazed and shocked. He calls me many times that day and night from a cell with many men and he is afraid and wants me to arrange for a $350 bail on $3,500. However, when he appears at the bond hearing on Saturday morning, the court lawyer is Ron Sanderson who knows Paul very well from the past and he asks the judge to keep Paul there for a psychological evaluation. This is to be done before the arraignment on February 25 or 28. Paul is very upset as he never thought this could happen to him. He is taken to jail. The rules are hard... I can visit only Friday and Sunday evening from 7:00-10:00, but not until next week. He is allowed only one call per day and I can bring only clothes and those only once a month, with a limit of two of each item. When I speak with Paul on Sunday and Monday he is much more calm although they do not give him any medication as yet even though it was sent with the detective from CHI on 2/9—25 mg Hydroxyzine twice a day per Dr. Porter.

2/83 – Paul catches scabies due to lack of cleanliness and is taken to the infirmary to be isolated as these sores are highly contagious. Then his cheeks swell and they think he has the mumps. When I brought clothes to him for some reason they were delayed in getting them to him so he wore the same outfit for a week. He returns to his cell which is shared by many men... lights are on twenty-four hours and a TV is going constantly. Paul develops a schedule where he sleeps during the day and remains awake at night. When I visit him with Phillip or Claudia or alone, we see him through a window and speak through a little slot. He has lost weight and there are still little scratch marks from the scabies, but his eyes are clear and although he has received no medication, he is doing fairly well. He has only a few sets of clothes to change per allotment and washes these by hand. He hopes that at the arraignment time he will be allowed to come home but Ron tells me they will undoubtedly ask for hospital commitment for a time, and this will be Chattahoochee unless he has other insurance. Dr. Azor tells me that Chattahoochee might be all right for only a month or two but that longer may be harmful... Dr. Davidson says that Chattahoochee is merely a holding station with little or no therapeutic value. He says that

Paul could be admitted under Medicare if the courts agree. Coverage for a psychiatrist is limited to a lifetime of some 100+ days, with first admittance up to sixty days, then break of another sixty days will erase the first.

3/4/83 – Paul appears before Judge Dea who accepts Ron Sanderson's recommendation and has Paul committed to Highland Park instead of Chattahoochee. Paul asks the judge if he can go home for the weekend but is denied. Paul remains in the jail while paperwork is done for the transfer.

3/16/83 – Highland Park – Paul is admitted. I paid the $317 deductible for the hospital which will be paid 100%. The doctor will be paid 80% and we will pay the balance. We pray that the sixty days will stabilize Paul and that he will cooperate. Since he is there through the courts, he cannot go on weekly outings nor earn passes to come home on weekends, but he is happy to be out of jail, which he found as a bad experience.

The main theme at Highland is group therapy and there are sessions a few times daily. Paul also takes part in doing ceramics and shooting pool. There is a friendly atmosphere and Family Nights on Tuesday, when patients sing or recite poetry. Paul is friendly but jokes in sessions and is shy to speak of himself and says he does not know what to speak about. There is no physical recreation nor does he go outside for sun and air. Occasionally he gets antsy and calls everyone... family, lawyers, friends... and tries to make deals to assure that he will have the two counts against him dropped. One is for the theft from Frank McCourt (two speakers, TV, and watch were not returned). The other is for conspiracy in the drug count against Bobby.

4/14/83 – Dr. Cameron is Paul's doctor who is on two weeks' vacation. I never spoke with him and only once with Victor (counselor). I finally reached Victor and was shocked to hear him say that he felt they had done all they could for Paul and planned to have him go to court the following Wednesday. He thought he would be committed to Chattahoochee, which he felt was best to further stabilize Paul and to keep him from returning to his old ways and to possibly be hurt for his drug connection, and maybe even killed. I was surprised since I had felt Paul was improved and that thirty days more would be even more helpful. In addition, I could not understand a counselor making this decision rather than a doctor.

4/15/83 – I called Dr. Davidson who had not been aware that Paul was in the hospital. He was surprised at the conversation I had with Victor and said that it would indeed be a mistake for him either to go to jail or to Chattahoochee. He added that he would speak with Dr. Cameron and that he would be back to me on Tuesday. Ron Sanderson, Paul's public defender, said he was surprised that Victor had reached such a decision and added that if he was taken to court on Wednesday that they would ask for a "speedy trial" which would keep him in jail at least two or three weeks. We were both pleased that Dr. Davidson had denied Victor and no further court date was set.

4/19/83 – Dr. Davidson called from his office where he was meeting with Dr. Cameron. Apparently Dr. Cameron was still unaware of Victor's decision and the call to me. Dr. Cameron was very upset and agreed with Davidson that Paul should be kept the sixty days and that he had indeed improved.

4/28/83 – I continue to visit Paul on Tuesday—Family Night—and on the weekends and so on. We speak a few times a day and he is in better condition than he has been in years. There was a meeting with Dr. Cameron, Victor, Paul, and me... the problem is that Ron Sanderson does not answer calls nor messages left for him and time is growing close to Paul's stay at Highland. Dr. Cameron feels that he would do well on an outpatient basis and that state institutes would be harmful. He seems encouraged by Paul's present condition. Ron is in court all week on a murder trial and will not answer our calls. Finally the hospital reaches a social worker at the jail, Jackie Arnold, who says she will contact doctors and she sets a court hearing for Monday, May 10.

5/10/83 – Judge Dea's court – Dr. Cameron appears with Paul as they have been advised that the court intends to send Paul to jail this weekend and to Chattahoochee next week. Father John Luzska also appears in Paul's behalf and Ron is also there. However, the judge says he needs psychological re-evaluations and not from Dr. Cameron, and schedules a hearing for Friday, May 13. Jackie Arnold will present a plan, which will have Paul in a program called Passageways which is for people who have been criminally involved. This rehabilitates them and helps with vocations. A bus would pick him up daily and return him home. We hope the evaluations will lead Judge Dea to rule in Paul's favor.

5/13/83 – Judge Dea has received two evaluations from Dr. Weiss and from one of the two evaluators in February. He agrees to release Paul on an outpatient basis under Passageways. He is to appear in court on June 20 to check on his progress.

Highland Park – Dr. Cameron signs the release for Paul and gives him five prescriptions: two before meals so his stomach will not be upset, one for a boil infection, Benadryl at night, and the fifth to be take two times per day. The doctor tells Paul to watch out very carefully that he does not get into trouble again and not go back to his old ways.

Paul is very happy to be home and has a girlfriend, Joanne, whom he met in Highland Park and who is studying to be a nurse's aid. In the first five days she is over twice and he is very pleased. He comes to Mass with us and to Bayfront Park with Claudia and helps around the house.

5/18/83 – Passageways – By agreement with Lee Edwards at Passageways, Paul is picked up and taken for an interview with Corinne, a counselor at Passageways. She advises that he can go to school at Fairchild Vocational School for mechanics, nurse's aid, etc. or go to Passageways each day with others just out of jail... who sit around and have outings to parks, movies, etc. We are disappointed as this is not the daily therapy we had been told about. Ron Sanderson called to check on Paul and advised me that they are keeping Paul "incompetent to stand trial" due to a "conflict of interest" in assigning two of their own attorneys on the same case. If all goes well with the conspiracy on the drug case, Paul will be let off; otherwise, an outside attorney will be hired by the courts. Bobby will be sentenced next week... if guilty, fifteen years in prison (seven and a half for good behavior). Most of McCourt's stuff has been returned so that charges will probably be dropped.

5/18/83 – After an absence of three months, Paul returns to CHI to receive first of weekly 37.5 mg (1.5 cc) Prolixin injection. The doctor is not there but Dave Byrd gets permission on the beeper and someone else gives the injection. All is well and Paul is enthused about attending Fairchild Vocational School, which we visited the previous day. The mechanic's course would cost $85 each semester. He does not want me to drive him but insists on going with a friend, John. He is quite nervous and goes to two stores to cash checks even though I tell him it is too late to register. He simply will not listen. He does not call nor return home during the evening, but rather some time in the middle of the night. He spent the entire $85 mostly at a bar, on drinks. I am furious and report it to the Passageways people who say there is a chance they will have him live there full time if we can get his medical records. During the next few days he settles down and tries to get a job at the barber shop to clean up, at a sub sandwich shop, etc. but has no luck. It will be best if he attends CHI for group each morning, or to Passageways a few days a week. They have an hour group at 10:00 each morning but that is the extent of the therapy. We are now waiting for either some part time work or one of these programs.

5/26/83 – CHI – Dr. Porter does not feel that Paul needs 1.5 cc of Prolixin and orders injections of either 1 cc or a ½.cc. Dr. Davidson is amazed that they do not continue with the dosage, which was established to keep him on a proper balance.

6/83 – Paul bides his time with a little work around the yard and house. He does one job for a Chattahoochee driveway which he does not quite finish since we cannot find the necessary sealer although we spend a few hours on a Saturday trying to locate it. He also cuts grass to earn a few dollars. He is sometimes low in spirit and occasionally tense. One evening we even get into the car to go to the VA but he changes his mind.

6/22/83 – Court – Claudia takes Paul to court where Judge Dea advises him that he had better shape up through Corinne at Passageways and with Ron and give 100% cooperation or the judge will be angry with him. Ron advises Paul that he could go to jail, the stockade, or Chattahoochee if he does not cooperate.

6/23/83 – CHI – No doctor available so Paul does not get an injection that week. He is all wound up and does not sleep well. He has plans galore and is full of stress.

7/1/83 – Social Security check arrives and Paul insists he can finance a car or truck with $200 down. He comes into the office to get a check and spends it the same day. At this time we find that he has stolen Claudia's gold bracelet, which her boyfriend had given to her. He received $30 for it at Interstate Gold and Coin Exchange. They later say they have already given it to be melted down and cannot help us. After telling him that he could not stay at home until he returned the bracelet as well as paying $50 per week, he tried to admit himself to the VA but they would not take him.

7/2/83 – Highland Park – Paul admitted himself on Saturday and signed out on Sunday. He used up his fifty-ninth and sixtieth days and did not want to stay on. He returned home and for the next few nights sleeps on a lounge chair.

7/5/83 – Paul gets a $2,500 stone job across the street at some new neighbors. I take him shopping for $150 for tools and early the next morning for sand and cement materials. The man pays for the stone himself upon delivery ($500.00 each time). At first, Paul is enthused and then starts hiring his raunchy friends to help. He starts drinking and doing his drugs and spending what he earns. I tell him to save his money in order to get an apartment and move out when the job is over.

7/11/83 – Paul picks up $100 check from me, which I held from his check for Claudia's bracelet. He says he is going to pick it up for her but spends it instead.

7/12/83 – Court – Judge Dea still lists Paul as incompetent to stand trial as there is a conflict of interest. In the hope that the other drug trial will be over, his next court date is October 5. I now want him only to sleep in the house and to stay out till I return at 5:30 after work. Dan takes Jillian each day as he does not want to remain home with Paul and his drug friends around. When Paul realizes that he has underbid the stone job and that he cannot finish it alone, he walks off the job. Four others finish it for the remainder of the $300–$400. He owes money out to some of the workers, which he does not have.

7/83 – One evening Paul is arrested at the park at US 3 and 14th Street for possession of a joint. He says they had no right to search him and will plead not guilty to the misdemeanor.

8/83 – He spends his days by occasionally working at Lum's early in the morning to get a free breakfast. He worked half a day for Doug Small then said he could not work anymore.

8/5/83 – CHI Paul and I waited an hour and a half as Dr. Porter was on vacation and no doctor was available. Dave Byrd was the only counselor and he had a patient with him. When Dr. Pearl was finally reached he would not okay Prolixin for Paul saying it was too late in the day! Which was not our fault as we had waited all that time and had been coming at 5:30 for four years!

8/10/83 – CHI Paul goes by bus for weekly Prolixin clinic and receives a 1.5 cc shot plus prescription to last two weeks for Benadryl (50mg) and another prescription. He is becoming more belligerent and at one point takes two of my checks but gives them back to me before trying to cash them. Social Security check for $376 goes very quickly... $150 owed to Claudia for bracelet and radio ($25), monies owed, and only $100 for house instead of $200. However, he insists on taking a check for the $100 and I tell him he can no longer stay at home. Instead of spending for himself, he buys $72 in groceries, taking a cab home from Kwick Check. He is in the house when I am there but in an effort to make him either work or go into the CHI program I lock him out of the house during the day.

8/12/83 – VA hospital – Paul breaks into the house by using a knife at the front door lock, takes what he says are thirty Thorazine pills, partly says because he cannot stand itching and partly because he cannot stand life. He did this early in the morning but does not call me until 4:00 in the afternoon when an ambulance driver is at the house and says Paul should wait for me to come home. When I arrive we go to the VA and Dr. Fisher, psychiatrist, admits him. A very kind doctor who takes the time to talk with me and explain that the very nature of Paul's illness is such that he cannot cope with many situations like we can and that even a mosquito bite can cause great stress. He said that even though Paul threw up after taking the pills, he doubts that he took such a large quantity. Dr. Fisher says that Paul probably can't work for any length of time and regardless what I do, he will go his way. He feels that it would be good for Paul to go to Chattahoochee, which is not as bad as described and that six months there would help a great deal. He also asked why the VA did not try lithium over a period of time.

8/15/83 – Court – I cancelled Paul's appearance before Judge Diamante for possession of a joint and they will reschedule later.

8/17/83 – Vocational Rehabilitation – Scott Saunders calls to say he has been trying to reach Paul to have him see Dr. Carroll for a psychological appraisal before doing the paperwork to get him into their program. I make the mistake of telling this to Paul who then signs himself out of the VA, AMA, and refuses to go back in. I tell him he cannot come back unless he works or goes into a program. He sleeps outside but goes to work at Lum's to earn breakfast and lunch. He then is allowed to sleep in the house but is restricted to the garage and outside when no one is home in the day.

8/25/93 – Dr. Carroll gives Paul three and a half hours of testing. The results will be sent to Vocational Rehabilitation and they will advise us.

8/27/83 – Doug Small hires Paul at $50 per day to mix for brick work and promises more when he does stone work. Paul works Saturday, Monday, Tuesday, and on Wednesday he walks off the job to go to CHI, saying his hands are raw and sore from the hoe and that he cannot work.

9/1/83 – Claudia and I go shopping with Paul in Dadeland and get him a pair of great pants at Burdine's and we have a lovely evening. The following day, Friday, he goes to Homestead with Frank McCourt to spend the day and meet a girl. He gives Frank $30 for the speakers he stole and has $50 for himself. This is from his September check. During the day he is attacked by two pit bull dogs. The police check and verify that they have had their rabies shots. He says he drank too much later and spent the night at McCourt's, returning home on Saturday.

9/3/83 – Claudia finds that her father's CB radio is missing. Paul admits giving it to a friend to "hold" until he pays $40 that he owes. I give him the money from the $100 money for September rent ($72 last month) and he returns the CB. Claudia is terribly disappointed with him, especially in view of the effort she was putting into helping him of late, and she speaks of a lock on her door or moving out. He says he had planned to return it when he had extra money to retrieve.

9/4/83 – We have a birthday party/Labor Day celebration and Paul is a great help and has a wonderful time. The following day he has a letdown and in the evening when we smell gas from his room he admits to sniffing lighter fluid to get a "high." This is Monday, Labor Day.

9/6/83 – Because of the theft and his actions the previous night, I restrict Paul from the house during the day. He gets a ride to my office, insists on the balance of his house money saying he is going to find a place to live. When I arrive home, I find he has broken into the house through a window and has spent $38 on drugs and liquor. I tell him he cannot come into the house. He calls the police who say they will not drive him to the VA hospital nor to CHI with taxpayers' money. He advises Paul to take his clothes and leave and that if he returns they will arrest him for trespassing. I give him seventy-five cents for the bus since he has nothing from the $38.

9/6-9/9/83 – CHI – Paul remains in the crisis unit for seventy-two hours. They will not let him leave AMA and I am called in the second day for consultation with a counselor and Paul. I say he cannot come home unless he attends the day program, which he refuses to do. Finally, in order to return home, he agrees to return to the CHI program for orientation on Wednesday.

9/13/83 – Paul meets with an attorney to see about suing the man who owns the pit bulls who attacked him. A rep from the attorney's office goes with Paul to Homestead to take pictures and has Paul set up an appointment with a doctor. However, Paul has two wisdom teeth pulled and is in pain and does not keep the appointment.

9/14/83 – CHI – Paul starts on the program and is to be picked up by bus each morning at 7:30. He is not enthused but attends.

9/21/83 – Court – Case before Judge Diamante is dismissed as police officer doesn't show up. This was for possession of a joint.

9/26/83 – While I am in Europe for two weeks, Paul is to attend CHI day program and money is left with Claudia for him on a daily basis as well as a check for weekly Prolixin injections, plus $25 for 10/3 when his Social Security check comes in. He attends on and off the first week, but stops going on Friday. Dan tells him he will have to stay out if he will not attend CHI as agreed. So Paul moves out and everything falls apart for him.

10/3/83 – Paul comes into my office at work and demands his check from Thomas, even calling in a policewoman saying that he only wants to "hold" the check until my return. Thomas says that he is a bum and will not give him the check and adds that if he returns he will be arrested. During the rest of the week he sleeps under a bridge and gets food from working at Lum's and doing odd jobs. One day he calls Claudia at Blue Lakes Elementary where she is working a few hours daily and says the house has been broken into and the silver stolen. Police are called in and Dan says that it is Paul who stole the silver and says he will press charges if not returned. It is returned all except for the sugar bowl and cover, which no one can locate. Dan tells him to stay off of the property, which he does until my return.

10/10/83 – Upon my return home I follow the rules and do not let him in since he has not worked nor is he attending CHI as agreed. He sleeps outside on a cot, goes to work at Lum's each morning for food, and I give him one meal outside in the evening. Claudia is extremely upset by all of this and especially by his previous week's behavior and is afraid of him.

9/23-9/28/83 – Gastroenterologist sees Paul because of his constant upset stomach and does tests on him ($798) – GI series with small bowel, pan upper endoscopy, etc. He was to return to finish testing but was locked out of the house and could not get medicines of pre-testing nor money for bus to go to the doctor's. Will schedule for a later date per doctor's instructions. Apparently, it is not an ulcer.

9/83-10/83 – Podiatrist saw Paul in regard to a dog bite on foot, which had become infected. He prescribed Duricef ($35), which Dan had some of but would not give any to help Paul. The primary reason he went to the doctor was not for pain but to comply with the attorney in order to settle a lawsuit in his favor.

10/19/83 – VA hospital – After sleeping outside for two weeks, working at odd jobs, sleeping on the floor at Frank McCourt's, Paul missed three Prolixin injections and was feeling low. Admitted himself to VA where he is given a 4 cc injection of Prolixin on 10/20/83.

*** Paul encounters additional run-ins with the law and, as a result, is evaluated and later committed to the forensic unit at Florida State Hospital in Chattahoochee, Florida, for a few years. The situation is no better there and as Claudia periodically visits she becomes extremely worried and upset. He has become violent at times and also has been in many fights with patients as well as staff members.

*** Upon release from the hospital, Paul returns home where the cycle continues with no help or sign of improvement. In 1988, Paul is placed at the forensic unit at South Florida State Hospital in Pembroke Pines, Florida. Claudia lives a short distance from the hospital and is able to visit him many times per week. Paul has become a "voice" of those on his ward, writing about the injustices he and others face there. Claudia signs him out occasionally on overnight passes and tries to improve his lifestyle as she is devastated with the conditions she sees him living in. At one visit, she is with Paul outside in the early evening hours eating some goodies she has brought. She looks up and notices a patient masturbating while he is watching her through a large glass window. In an effort not to alarm Paul who has his back to the window, Claudia continues her visit but is reluctant to return again.

PART THREE
THE DOCTORS' STORY

Psychological Evaluations

Neurology Electrodiagnosis
Theodore Hoekstra, M.D., P.A.
Diplomate, American Board of Neurology
Peter S. Becker, M.D.

Neurological Consultation
Paul Maurer
February 18, 1981

The patient is a 22-year-old right-handed white male who was accompanied by his mother to the office. Apparently the patient has had psychiatric problems for at least the past two years or so. He has been hospitalized at the Veterans Administration Hospital and does state that at least for the past year, he has heard voices and been able to communicate with God. He continues to have for the past year headaches involving the vertex area. Five years ago, he fell on the back of his head without any loss of consciousness and within the past week, was hit over the head with an iron by his brother because of the patient's insistence on procuring money from his brother. Apparently, there have been problems with drugs in the past, which the patient freely admits to. He is currently followed at CHI and on bi-weekly Prolixin injections. He does not see a psychiatrist regularly. He also has had episodes of hyperventilation with tingling in the feet and in the hands, but no other neurological symptoms. The patient also has a partial traumatic amputation of one of his fingers from an on-the-job forklift accident. He smokes two packs of cigarettes per day and also consumes alcohol. He had an electroencephalogram read by Dr. Becker on the ninth of this month, which was considered borderline, due to excessive theta activity with possible contribution from drowsiness. The patient was in the armed forces for about somewhat over a year several years ago and apparently had behavior problems in the service. His biological father from whom his mother is divorced also has had extensive problems with alcohol and apparently psychiatric problems as well. There are several other siblings who have no psychiatric problems whatsoever and there is no history of advential movement disorder in the patient or in the family.
 NEUROLOGICAL EXAMINATION: The patient is alert and oriented X3. There is no receptive or expressive aphasia. There is

Claudia M. Jones Ph.D.

a mild dysarthria. **CRANIAL NERVES:** Pupils are equal, round, and reactive and consensually. Fundi are normal. Visual fields are full to confrontation. Palpebral fissures are equal. The range of extracurricular movements is full without nystagmus. Facial sensation and hearing are normal. There is no masticatory, facial, palatal or lingual weakness. **REFLEXES:** Biceps, triceps, patellar and Achilles deep tendon reflexes are 2+ bilaterally. Plantar responses are flexor. **MOTOR EXAMINATION:** Muscle, bulk, tone and strength are normal. **SENSORY EXAMINATION:** Position and superficial pain sensation are intact. **COORDINATION, GAIT AND STATION:** Coordination, gait and station are normal. Blood pressure in the right arm is 120/70.

IMPRESSION: PSYCHOGENIC CEPHALGIA
PROBABLE AMBULATORY SCHIZOPHRENIC

I have suggested to the patient's mother that in view of his recent trauma and the continuing headaches over the past year as well as the extensive psychiatric history, that the patient have a CT scan plain and contrast of the brain. She is not in a financial position to have this scan obtained privately but will attempt to have it performed at the VA, but the patient does not remain in the hospital long enough for it to be completed. The patient is discharged and is referred back to the Veterans Administration and CHI facilities and physicians.

Theodore Hoekstra, M.D.

Leonard P. Eugene, Ph.D.
Psychologist

April 4, 1981

Psychological Evaluation

To: Honorable Albert S. Dea Circuit Court – Criminal
Re: Paul G. Maurer

Dear Judge Dea,

Pursuant to your request, Paul G. Maurer was seen for a psychological evaluation to determine his mental status and render an opinion as to his competency to stand trial. It was also requested to determine whether or not he was sane at the time of the alleged offense as well as render an opinion to his prognosis and psychiatric treatment. Mr. Maurer was charged with burglary and grand theft. He was seen at my office in Miami, Florida. At the time of the assessment he was in custody of his mother.

Mr. Maurer is a twenty-three year old white male who came to the interview accompanied by his mother. He is one of four siblings, two brothers and a sister. He is second to the youngest. His parents were divorced when he was thirteen. He sees his father once in a while. According to him, his grandmother has emotional problems and defines his relationship with his siblings to be poor.

In discussing his physical health, Mr. Maurer related that he has a difficult time maintaining a job because he appears to require "a lot of sleep." He complained of having bad headaches, back pain, sharp pains in his chest, and sweating palms. According to him, at times he cannot move his hands for about five minutes. Every night he finds himself itching his leg.

Educationally, Mr. Maurer has completed the tenth grade. Work history includes cutting stone. According to Mr. Maurer he supported himself through trying to get Social Security. He has a long standing history of drug addiction. This includes acid, cocaine, and marijuana. He has had previous charges, which include arson and burglary; however, he has never been convicted.

Test rapport was easily established. He was highly cooperative and responsive to the tasks that were required of him. There was a tendency to be compulsive in his verbal responses. Excessive sweating was noted.

The following tests were administered: Bender-Gestalt, Bender-Gestalt Recall, House-Tree-Person (Chromatic and Achromatic), portions of the Wechsler Adult Intelligence Scale, Animal Test, Free Drawing Test, and the Rorschach.

Mr. Maurer was oriented in time, place, and person. His affect seemed to be appropriate to his thought content. Loose association and perceptual distortions were evident. He seems to be functioning within the dull normal range of intelligence with a limited fund of knowledge and introspective ability. He used projection as main defense mechanism. Mr. Maurer appeared to be actively psychotic.

Mr. Maurer's psychotic state seems to permeate throughout his intellectual, emotional, and individual expressions. He appears to have gathered very little of the so-called general information from the environment that one would expect from individuals who live in this culture. He does not seem to be able to generalize adequately a sample of past behavior and apply it to a newly developed social situation. He appears to be poorly acculturated into the mainstream of society, particularly in the sphere of moral and ethical judgment.

Common sense, adequate judgment, and competence in dealing with the social environment is marginally developed. His comprehension and capacity for associative thinking is slightly below the average range. It seems that when he is able to control his internal noise, his concentration and alertness to his environment increases. His problem- solving skills are marginal. He appears to decompensate in a face of environmental complexity.

Mr. Maurer's behavior is typified by a paranoid delusional system of persecution. He sees himself as the object of FBI surveillance because "they think I'm heavy." His involvement with drugs is seen by him as a source of his mind's deterioration and its ineffectiveness. According to him, the LSD that he has taken was dripping into his brain, splitting "my mind apart." Such an event caused part of his mind to be taken away by the people who offered him the drugs.

His test results further suggest poor planning ability and inability to adhere to a systematic order in his life. Emotional fluctuation, variability, inner confusion, and unpredictability dominate his psychological style. Impulsivity and aggressive-hostile tendencies characterize his relationships with the social environment. Sporadic loss of control is possible. During such times, he can become belligerent and abusive.

Summary and Conclusion

Given my present clinical understanding of this case, and within reasonable psychological probability, I find Mr. Paul Maurer to exhibit behaviors which are similar to those individuals who are psychologically diagnosed as schizophrenic, paranoid type. Apparently he has a long-standing psychiatric history which include several admissions to the VA hospital. He appeared to be a loosely put together individual, with marginal coping skills and adaptive resources. Although he is actively psychotic, he seems to be able to manage his life outside of hospital settings. However, he will decompensate under moderate stress.

As to his competency to stand trial, I am of the opinion that Mr. Paul Maurer is marginally competent.

As to his sanity at the time of the alleged offense, I am of the opinion that Mr. Maurer was insane. He marginally knew right from wrong but did not understand the nature and the consequence of his actions.

As to his mental condition as it affects his competency, I am of the opinion that with the exception of his motivation to help himself in the legal process, he is competent.

As to his psychiatric prognosis and treatment, I am of the opinion that his prognostic future is moderate. Treatment within a therapeutic community (outside of a hospital setting) is recommended. His treatment should include antipsychotic medication, individual, and group psychotherapy. Vocational training will be helpful in effort to increase his self-esteem.

I trust that this information is of value to you. If you have any questions, please do not hesitate to call on me.

Sincerely,

Leonard P. Eugene, Ph.D.

Claudia M. Jones Ph.D.

VETERANS ADMINISTRATION APPEAL
TO BOARD OF VETERANS APPEALS

RE: MAURER, Paul G.
Date of decision being appealed: March 6, 1981

I hereby petition the Board of Veterans Appeals for relief as set forth below:

Request for Medical Help

Paul entered Marines at 17 in good physical and mental health. In service was treated for alcohol problems, spent time in brig, recommended for psychiatric help, which he declined. Discharge to adjusting; nerves, at very least.

After return home problems increased. We were unaware of help until extreme mental disorder admitted him to V.A. Hospital twice under Baker Act and ex parte. Inpatient (not mentioned in your report) 4 or 5 times. Dr. Azor, head of psychiatry at V.A. is familiar with Paul.

1.) Dr. Hoekstra, neurologist, has seen Paul and is to send report to you. 2.) Dr. Ivans, psychiatrist, filed his report with Soc. Sec. Both refer to "long standing mental problems," which seem likely to date back to Marine days. They attest to need for medical help (psychiatry) in order to function in society. 3.) For few years Paul received Prolixin shots at CHI Clinic. They now suggest shock treatments not provided there.

Paul has been able to work less and less as headaches and hallucinations increase. He tries to do odd jobs which last a day or two. Anyone seeing or talking to him would not hire him. When under great stress walks into hospitals and doctors' offices although he has not a cent nor any hospitalization insurance.

If a hearing is advised, please let us know. If more details or information is desired, please advise. Thank you kindly.

Sophia Maurer
on behalf of Paul G. Maurer

IN THE APPEAL OF PAUL G. MAURER

FEBRUARY 8, 1982

BOARD OF VETERAN'S APPEALS
WASHINGTON, D.C. 20420

FINDINGS AND DECISION

THE ISSUE

Entitlement to a service connection for a psychiatric disorder.

CONTENTIONS

It is contended that the veteran was in good physical and mental health when he entered the service, and during service he was treated for alcohol problems, spent some time in the brig, and was recommended for psychiatric help, which he declined. After his return home his problems increased. He has been hospitalized for psychiatric treatment since his discharge from the service.

THE EVIDENCE

The veteran served from April 1976 to August 1977.

Service and post-service medical records on file show no treatment, complaints, or findings indicative of a nervous or psychiatric disorder, either during service or within one year after discharge. The last examination report in service, dated in July 1977, noted the psychiatric system as normal.

A nervous disorder is initially shown by medical evidence on file in April 1979, when the veteran was admitted to a Veterans Administration hospital under the Baker Act and remained approximately three days. He left before a full evaluation could be done. The reason for admission was noted to be bizarre behavior. The diagnosis was rule out acute schizophrenic episode.

Reports of subsequent medical treatment are on file. In November 1979, the diagnostic impressions included schizophrenia, rule out toxic psychosis secondary to PCP use, or organic brain syndrome due to PCP.

Claudia M. Jones Ph.D.

The veteran's mother, in May 1980, wrote a letter to the effect that her son had joined the Marines at the age of 17, and had been delighted and enthusiastic. When he returned 15 months later, he was an unhappy and sick young man. He had not been able to work more than 1 or 2 weeks at a time. He had been in a Veterans Administration hospital a number of times in the psychiatric ward. She further indicated that the only physicians who had treated her son were those in the service and in the Veterans Administration hospital.

THE LAW AND REGULATIONS

Service connection may be granted for disability resulting from disease or injury incurred in or aggravated by peacetime service. (38 U.S.C 331)

Where a veteran served continuously for ninety (90) days or more during a period of war or during peacetime service after December 31, 1946, and a psychosis becomes manifest to a degree of ten percent (10%) within one year from date of termination of such service, such disease shall be presumed to have been incurred in service, even though there is no evidence of such disease during the period of service. This presumption is rebuttable by affirmative evidence to the contrary. (38 U.S.C. 312, 313, 337; 38 C.F.R. 3.307)

DISCUSSION AND EVALUATION

While it is contended that the veteran manifested symptoms of a nervous disorder during service, and from the time of his discharge from service, the available service and post-service medical records do not substantiate these contentions, and show no pertinent manifestations until more than one year after service.

The determination of the Board is based primarily on the objective evidence, and must be in accordance with applicable provisions of the law and regulations. All reasonable doubt is resolved in favor of the claimant. However, in this case, there is no reasonable basis shown for concluding that the veteran's nervous disorder, first shown by the medical evidence approximately 20 months after service, had its onset in service, or that it meets the criteria for service connection under the presumptive provisions of the cited law and regulations.

FINDINGS OF FACT

1. A psychiatric disorder is not shown by the pertinent evidence to have been present in service.
2. A psychiatric disorder, variously diagnosed, is not shown by medical evidence currently on file to have been manifested until approximately 20 months following the veteran's discharge from service.

CONCLUSIONS OF LAW

1. A psychiatric disorder was not incurred in or aggravated by service. (38 U.S.C. 331)
2. A psychosis was not manifested to a degree of ten percent (10%) or more within the resumptive one-year period following discharge from service. (38 U.S.C. 312, 313, 337; 38 C.F.R. 3.307)

DECISION

Entitlement to service connection for a psychiatric disorder is not established. The benefit sought on appeal is denied.

R.P. Morris
J.R. North, M.D.
K.J. Lewis

Claudia M. Jones Ph.D.

Alex Hallenborg, Ph.D., P.A.
Clinical Psychologist
Diplomate, American Board of Forensic Psychology

February 23, 1983

Honorable John Menadier
Judge, Eleventh Judicial Court
Miami, Florida
Re: Paul G. Maurer

Dear Sir,

The above-named individual was provided a psychodiagnostic examination, this date, as ordered at the Dade County Jail. There was apparent rapport, with articulate participation and it is believed that the findings derived are valid and representative of this individual at this time.

Personal Narrative:

This twenty-four year old Miamian began a stream of speech that was necessary to interrupt frequently to obtain information from him. He reports that he has been arrested for various charges of Breaking and Entering, Possession of a Controlled Substance and that this is the only time that he has been confined for more than overnight. There were two arrests as a juvenile, one for having thrown an incendiary device onto another youngster's driveway because of nonpayment of a $500 debt.

Also reported were thirty or more hospitalizations, most recently at the Veterans Hospital and at Highland Park General for his experiences of hallucinations, which he describes as experiences of extrasensory perceptions. Some of his hospital confinements were related, also, to substance abuses with some fifty events of LSD usage admitted.

This defendant's family, according to him, physically abused him since early childhood and have been among the many persons who have reportedly betrayed his trust and have been unwilling to believe his tales of surrealistic inventions.

His education was terminated at the ninth grade because of his desire to pursue his intended trade of "stoneworker" which he has followed since age fourteen. He views his present work as that of an "inventor."

He is now under medication, except that he has not received his weekly injection since being confined for the past two weeks. He feels this medication is essential to behavior control.

Observations:

This individual displays intense pressure of speech, delusions of grandiosity and deep concern that his rationality is questioned. Although he exhibits an overt effort at personal control, his remarks reflect a potential for violent behavior. His level of intelligence is in the above-average/superior range and his perceptions of reality indicate an acute, although distorted, awareness of his environment and his interactions with people. The psychodiagnostic test data are consistent with a diagnosis of chronic schizophrenia with paranoidal ideation.

Summary:

It is my clinical opinion that Paul Maurer is now experiencing a major mental illness, schizophrenia, as he has been for many years. There is also a possibility of an organic brain syndrome resulting from the prolonged usage of hallucinogenic substances.

While he verbalizes an appreciation of the charges against him and the range and nature of possible penalties, his distorted perceptions of reality regarding himself and his activities precludes his being able to assist counsel, answer charges against him or to stand trial.

The nature of his chronic thought disorder indicates that at the time of his alleged offense he was unable to know the difference between right and wrong or to know the nature and consequences of his acts.

The defendant's report of his role as a police informant is as bizarre as his other narratives about himself and reflects his own consistent belief in his unreality. Granting the validity of his reported treatment history, his confinement for a long-term hospitalization and treatment of his mental illness is indicated.

Claudia M. Jones Ph.D.

Prognosis is guarded for effective therapy. On the other hand, strong likelihood for his marginal social adjustment and underlying psychopathology producing new offenses exists.

I appreciate this opportunity to be of service to the Court.

Respectfully,
Alex Hallenborg, Ph.D.

Leonard P. Eugene, Ph.D.
Psychologist

The Professional Arts Center
Miami, Florida

February 25, 1983

RE: Paul G. Maurer

Dear Judge Milton:

Pursuant to your request, Mr. Paul Maurer was seen for a psychological evaluation to determine his mental status as it relates to his competency to stand trial. It was also requested to render an opinion as to whether or not he meets the criteria for involuntary hospitalization, as well as to his sanity at the time of the alleged offense. Mr. Maurer was charged with burglary and grand theft. However, these charges are suggested by Mr. Maurer. The statement of facts which was attached to the court order suggests his involvement in a drug conspiracy, trafficking in and possession of cocaine. Mr. Maurer was interviewed on February 18, 1983. At the time of his assessment, he was incarcerated at the Dade County Jail.

It is important to note that this examiner has evaluated Mr. Maurer on April 4, 1981, on different charges. At that time, Judge Dea ordered the psychological evaluation of the defendant. A complete overview of the defendant's background can be found in the court file.

Family history reveals that Mr. Maurer is one of four siblings, two brothers and one sister. According to him, his parents were divorced when he was at the age of 13. His father remarried. He last saw his father four months ago. According to him, at the time of his arrest, he was living with his mother.

I questioned him as to whether or not any individual in his family had suffered from emotional disturbance. He suggested that his grandmother suffered from deep depression.

Apparently Mr. Maurer is not married, he has a lot of girlfriends, but he suffers from lack of sexual drive.

Medical history was relatively unmarked. According to him, when he was about 16, he cut one of the fingers of his right hand,

Claudia M. Jones Ph.D.

as well as having had an accident during that time which resulted in a serious head injury. According to him, he suffers from pressure on his head, with pain shooting from the back to the front. He also complained of stomachache, constipation, and at times, diarrhea. He maintained that at times his vision gets blurry, he feels dizzy, and concentration is difficult.

Psychiatric history includes thirty episodes of hospitalization at the VA. The most recent one was three weeks ago. He also spent time in Highland Park a year and a half ago. According to him, his first admission was in 1979. The reason for his admission is because of his hearing voices and believing that guns are pointing at him.

Mr. Maurer joined the service in 1977. During boot camp he had his first nervous breakdown.

Educationally, he attended Killian High School and had completed the ninth grade. His drug history includes reefer, PCP, DPC, and acid.

Test rapport was easily established. Mr. Maurer recognized this examiner from a previous meeting. His outward appearance seemed to be somewhat neglected. He was unshaven, his shirt was bloody, and he was not wearing any shoes. At the time, he was suffering from the mumps.

The following tests were administered: the Bender Gestalt, the Bender Gestalt Recall, the house-tree-person test, chromatic and achromatic, portions of the Wechsler Adult Intelligence Skill, and the Rorschach.

Mr. Maurer was oriented in time, place, and person. He was surely not coherent, logical, nor goal directed. His affect was inappropriate, and did not follow his thought content. He had a tendency to delusion. His association is somewhat compulsive in his effect to talk. He seems to be flighty and fluctuating. He appears to be functioning within the dull-normal range of intelligence, with a limited fund of knowledge and introspective ability. It appears that he is poorly acculturated to the mainstream of culture. His ability to concentrate and to free himself from destructibility appears to be marginal. Common sense, judgment, and competence in dealing with his environment is moderate. His memory, recent and remote, appeared to be poor.

His present emotional state is typified by organized delusional system, whereby he sees himself as a messenger of God who is appointed to dissolve the DA, the FBI, and the CIA. He actually believes that he is part of the Secret Service, and he actually believes that he works for them. He complained of hearing voices throughout his life. These voices, according to him, are coming from the outside. He recognizes them and has names for these voices. Apparently, all of these voices are women's voices. According to him, they tease him all the time, and they play with his mind.

It appears that Mr. Maurer has decompensated further since the first psychological evaluation. At this point, he appears to have marginal hold on reality and to have serious deficiencies in dealing with his environment. Hostile aggressive tendencies dominate his clinical profile.

SUMMARY AND CONCLUSION:

Given my present clinical understanding of this case, and within reasonable psychological probability, I find Mr. Paul Maurer to be suffering from schizophrenia, paranoid type. His emotional disturbance has existed long before his present alleged offense. I am of the opinion that his intellectual, emotional, social behaviors are dominated by his delusional system, which appears to be quite composed and systematic. His reality adjusting is marginal. His defense mechanism can be easily pierced through, and further decompensation is probable.

As to whether or not he meets the criteria for involuntary hospitalization, I am of the opinion that Mr. Maurer does meet the criteria. I believe that, at this point, he needs to be returned to a helpful setting, whereby medical and psychiatric treatment is highly recommended. As to whether or not he was sane at the time of the alleged offense, I am of the opinion that Mr. Maurer was insane. He did not know right from wrong, nor did he understand the nature and the consequences of his actions. I believe that his behavior was dominated by his delusional system, and that he acted according to his set of internal beliefs.

Claudia M. Jones Ph.D.

I trust that this information is of value to you. If you have any questions, please do not hesitate to call me.

                                          Sincerely,
                                          Leonard P. Eugene, Ph.D.

NATHANIEL H. DENNIS, M.D.
Forensic Psychiatry

Diplomate
American Board of Psychiatry and Neurology
Coral Gables, Florida

May 11, 1983

Honorable Albert S. Dea
Miami, Florida
Re: Maurer, Paul

Dear Judge Dea,

Pursuant to your court order of May 10, 1983, I performed a psychiatric examination of Paul Maurer, 24, on the fourth floor of Highland Park General Hospital. The psychiatric examination of Paul Maurer took place on May 10, 1983. Mr. Maurer has been charged with burglary and grand theft, and conspiracy to traffic in narcotic substances (cocaine).

The examination was performed in order to determine whether or not Mr. Maurer had been restored to competence to stand trial. He was adjudicated mentally incompetent to stand trial on March 4, 1983. He was placed in Highland Park General Hospital on March 16, 1983. The staff at Highland Park General Hospital, including Dr. Gerald Cameron, believe that Mr. Maurer had regained his competence to stand trial, and felt further that he did not meet the criteria for hospitalization.

In the preparation of this psychiatric report I reviewed the defendant's medical record at Highland Park General Hospital and discussed his case briefly with his team leader and nurse.

Paul Maurer is an individual with a history of mental illness and hospitalization. He has been treated with electroshock therapy. He has been placed on antipsychotic medications. Most recently he has been a patient at the Community Mental Health Center of South Dade. He was under the care of Dr. Bruce Porter at the clinic. He has been determined to be mentally ill for the purpose of receiving Social Security disability benefits.

In addition to his history of mental illness Mr. Maurer has a history of drug abuse. He stated that he would discontinue using this drug as well as other drugs.

Mr. Maurer appeared to be knowledgeable about his legal predicament. He stated that he was charged with burglary and grand theft, and he claimed that he only took what was equivalent to a debt owed to him by his victim, Mr. Frank McCourt. Apparently he worked with Mr. McCourt as a stonemason, but Mr. McCourt discharged him from his duties and refused to pay for services rendered, a job about half complete.

He was in jail for these charges when additional charges were brought against him for conspiracy to sell or distribute cocaine. The truck drug trafficking charge came about because of Mr. Maurer's involvement in the selling of cocaine between Mr. Sheehan and undercover agents. Mr. Maurer stated that he had telephoned substation four in south Dade to determine whether or not the undercover agents were indeed police officers. It was his hope that Mr. Sheehan would be "busted" and arrested for cocaine possession or sale. He was told by Detective Locke that it was all right to engage in the transaction as long as he did not know where the drugs were being kept.

Mr. Maurer stated that he would "subpoena" Detective Locke to be a "material witness" at his trial, that Detective Locke would "testify" at the trial and would be subject to a "cross-examination" of the state attorney. It may be seen by the defendant's proper use of terms that he was knowledgeable about the workings of a court.

Further questioning revealed that Mr. Maurer knew the difference between a finding of guilt and of innocence, that he understood that a judge sentenced defendants found guilty, that a group of people who assisted the court constituted a "jury." He knew well that a person found guilty could go to jail or prison, but a person found innocent would be "released immediately."

Mr. Maurer gave the name of his attorney as Bill King, Assistant Public Defender. He also gave the name of an individual, an attorney that he used in attempting to gain compensation through the Veterans Administration as a service-connected veteran.

My interview with Paul Maurer led me to believe that he was no longer seriously psychotic. He was mentally ill, but stable on his antipsychotic medications. He could be released into outpatient treatment. He was well aware of his past history of treatment at the South Dade Community Mental Health Center, and he was comfortable with this referral.

If indeed Mr. Maurer is placed in the custody of his mother, he should by all means continue to go to CHI to receive medication management under the care of Dr. Porter. His medications include Prolixin decanoate 1.5 cc by injection every week. He also takes medicine for side effects and other medicines for stomach problems.

If Mr. Maurer is not adequately supervised, and resorts to the use of illicit drugs, then it is entirely possible that his mental condition will deteriorate once again.

The staff at the hospital has also suggested that Mr. Maurer be under the supervision of the Passageways Program. I was unaware that the Passageways Program provided support to individuals in the southern part of Dade County, but this support would be most useful to Mr. Maurer. An alternative would be referral to the Fellowship House Program or to CHI for day treatment program.

In my opinion, Paul Maurer is mentally <u>competent</u> to stand trial at the present time. He need not be maintained in a hospital environment, but could be treated under less restrictive alternatives. His medications have resulted in stabilization of his overall mental condition, but his mental condition is stable because of medication management primarily, and any substantial change in the use of medicine, or the addition of drugs or alcohol, would result in a worsening of his mental condition.

In my opinion, Paul Maurer could be released into outpatient psychiatric care under special circumstances and conditions, as outlined above.

Thank you very much for the opportunity to examine Paul Maurer.

Respectfully submitted,
Nathaniel H. Dennis, M.D.

Claudia M. Jones Ph.D.

NATHANIEL H. DENNIS, M.D.
Forensic Psychiatry

Diplomate
American Board of Psychiatry and Neurology
Coral Gables, Florida

Honorable Albert S. Dea
Miami, Florida
RE: Maurer, Paul

Dear Judge Dea:

Pursuant to your court order of October 24, 1983, I performed a psychiatric re-examination of Paul Maurer, 24, in the Dade County Jail. The psychiatric re-examination of Paul Maurer took place on October 26, 1983. Mr. Maurer has been charged with burglary and grand theft, and trafficking in illicit drugs.

In the preparation of this psychiatric report I reviewed the defendant's medical record in the Dade County Jail. In addition, I reviewed my previous psychiatric examination of Paul Maurer dated May 11, 1983.

Paul Maurer suffers from symptoms of a chronic mental disorder. He has been treated with antipsychotic medications for a period if many years. He has a history of drug abuse, and undoubtedly his drug abuse aggravated his unstable mental condition. He has been determined to be mentally disabled for the purpose of receiving Social Security disability benefits.

Mr. Maurer explained that he was in jail because the Passageways people felt that he should be examined by a psychiatrist. He gave no other reason for his placement in the jail. He did admit that he did not wish to go to the CHI program or to the Passageways Program on a daily basis. He also admitted that his mother kicked him out of the family home following her return from vacation. Apparently he had had some friends over to the house and had not continued to go see the Passageways staff.

On October 26, 1983, Paul Maurer was pleasant, verbal, and cooperative. He was relatively neat and clean, sporting a bandage over his ribcage following a fight which took place last night. He wore a pair of pinstripe pants and a white shirt which was open, but he had just come from the clinic. He smoked one cigarette. He did not wear shoes. His hair was short. He was clean shaven.

Paul demonstrated appropriate interpersonal behavior. He recognized me immediately and was pleasant and cooperative. He demonstrated no bizarre thought content. The only possible mental abnormality was his belief that he was going back into business and would be footing for jobs as a stonemason.

Mr. Maurer told me, "I think it's more therapeutic for me to work than to be in a program." This may be a realistic appraisal, or a rationalization for his non-cooperative attitude.

On October 26, 1983 Paul Maurer did not exhibit symptoms of mental illness or mental abnormality which would necessitate referral for psychiatric hospitalization. He may be treated on an outpatient basis at the Community Mental Health Center of South Dade.

Initially, I believe that placement in the Passageways Program would be useful to Paul Maurer. However, Paul lives in Kimball, goes to the CHI Clinic for medicine, and goes to North Dade to the Passageways Program for daily socialization. This may be confusing and disorganizing for Paul, insofar as he has numerous places to go for various treatments, perhaps contrary to his own desires. It might be more useful to have Paul go to one program nearer to his home than to two different programs.

In the event that his mother will allow him back into the family home, Paul should be allowed to return to the community and to maintain his status as a patient at the CHI Clinic under the care of Dr. Bruce Porter.

His present mental condition renders him mentally <u>competent</u> to stand trial. He does not require involuntary hospitalization under the Baker Act.

Thank you very much for the opportunity to re-examine Paul Maurer.

Respectfully submitted,
Nathaniel H. Dennis, M.D.

EPILOGUE

It has been nearly twenty years since I wrote the final entry in the journal I kept regarding my son Paul. He has indeed mellowed since that journal was written, and at the age of forty-three he is no longer constantly in trouble, in hospitals, or in great pain. As long as he receives a Prolixin injection every two to three weeks he remains stable and able to cope, although he is not able to work on a steady basis, nor can he manage his money or the day-to-day details of his life without assistance.

I love my four children, who make me quite proud. They have seven academic degrees among them, fine positions, and money in the bank. I have a heavy heart to think of all that Paul has missed in life—not degrees, status, or money in the bank, but rather the joys of a wife, children, a happy home of his own, friends, a job, a car... the daily life we take for granted.

I see a kindness and sweetness in Paul and am forever grateful to the many people who have been helpful to him over the years. And with all my heart, I thank those who continue to be patient and compassionate. His best friends are his sister, her husband, and their five children, with whom Paul finds warmth and love.

— Sofia Maurer